TALKING TURKEY

ROSTERS LTD.

TALKING TURKEY

Alison Rice

Rosters Ltd

Published by ROSTERS LTD.
60 Welbeck Street, London W1

© Alison Rice
Photographs Alison Rice
ISBN 0 9480 3238 3

First Edition 1989

This book is sold subject to the condition that it shall not, by way of trade or otherwise, be lent, re-sold, hired out or otherwise circulated without the publisher's prior consent in any form of binding or cover other than that in which it is published and without a similar condition being imposed on the subsequent purchaser.

All rights reserved. No part of this book may be reproduced or transmitted by any means without prior permission.

Every possible care has been taken to ensure the accuracy of the information in this book. The trouble with writing any guide book is that during the time it takes to write and print, places can change. Nowhere is this happening as fast as along the holiday coasts of Turkey. I hope I've anticipated the major possible changes but the publishers cannot accept responsibility for any errors or inaccuracies.

Designed and published by ROSTERS
Typeset by Gwynne Printers Ltd, Hurstpierpoint, Sussex
Printed and bound in Great Britain by Cox & Wyman Ltd, Reading

Acknowledgements

Compiling the information for this book was made a much easier task because of the good-natured and generous help offered to me by many people in the travel industry. I wish there was space to mention them all by name. I'd especially like to thank Vic Fatah of Redwing Travel and Bronwyn Gold Blyth of Scott Gold Blyth for their invaluable help and their honesty.

Thanks too to Ercihan Duzgunoglu of the Turkish Culture and Information Office in London for his very generous assistance.

This book was knocked into shape by Jeffery Pike whose talent and patience make him the very best of editors.

Above all I'm grateful to Turkey and the people of Turkey for being there.

Dedication

To my parents Brenda and Peter Rice.
They made all things possible.

Contents

Chapter One: The Guest Comes From God 11

Chapter Two: Choosing The Right Holiday 17

Chapter Three: What To Take With You 25

Chapter Four: Essential Information 31

Chapter Five: Holiday Health 39

Chapter Six: Getting Around 45

Chapter Seven: Shopping 53

Chapter Eight: Tasting Turkey 59

Chapter Nine: Istanbul 73

Chapter Ten: Resort Reports 87

Chapter Eleven: Excursions 109

Chapter Twelve: Messing About In Boats 129

Chapter Thirteen: Bluff Your Way Through
Turkish History 137

Chapter Fourteen: Talking Turkish 143

Chapter Fifteen: When Things Go Wrong 147

Chapter Sixteen: Who Goes Where 153

Index 189

CHAPTER ONE:
THE GUEST COMES FROM GOD

To listen to people in the holiday industry talk, you'd think that this great land mass we call Turkey had only just emerged from under the turquoise blue seas. No other country has developed a mass tourist industry quite so quickly as Turkey. No other stretch of coast has had to cope so fast with such large numbers of foreign visitors revelling in their "discovery" of an unspoilt, low-priced, hot, sunny country. Yesterday's shepherd's hut is today's guest house and restaurant – and tomorrow's hotel, disco and shopping plaza.

In only four summers, the farm labourer has moved along from letting the occasional German backpacker pitch a tent in his scrubby field to running a twenty-room bed and breakfast hotel. His brother might still be tilling land and his wife still spinning yarn, but his son is mixing pina coladas and learning to swear in three different languages. There's a concrete mixer where the donkey used to be, but his mother still bakes the family bread each morning – now with extra loaves for the holidaymakers.

Warm welcome

As anyone already smitten by Turkey's charm – and bitten by Turkey's mosquitoes – will tell you, this is the country to visit for a real sense of being abroad, a real taste of Asia; a country where it's still possible to feel welcome and where the locals consider that a holidaymaker is a guest and not a number on a clipboard. Heed the Turkish saying: "The guest comes from God." Most Turks do. Your accommodation might be basic, your conversations with the locals limited by language. You may fall asleep at night dreaming wistfully of baths and hot water, of dust-free towns and of roast beef and roast potatoes; but in Turkey you will touch a lifestyle which, over the last few thousand turbulent years, has changed very little. Until now.

Many of the most newly commercialised, Europeanised resorts on the Turkish coast are still a good few years away from offering wall-to-wall Wimpeys and Watneys. The men still gather in their cafes to discuss life, politics and football. The women still stoop double in the fields, picking stones from the soil and stacking the crops into stooks. The boys still run from shop to shop swinging trays of tiny glasses of hot mint tea. It all makes for a rare and fascinating mixture for the aware, interested holidaymaker.

Choice of resort

If you want a holiday with Mediterranean Riviera style, choose the right Turkish resort and you can find a place with more than a veneer of sophistication, where you can dress up at dusk and dance through till dawn to the beat of this summer's Western hits, and where your credit card will buy you designer leathers and fancy cocktails.

At the other extreme, you can choose a village where you'll be among the very first Britons to arrive as package holidaymakers; where you'll have to do a lot of pointing and smiling to communicate and you can teach the waiter's children (and perhaps the waiter) to say "hello", "how are you?" and "very good".

I bet you a pound of aubergines and my mosquito repellant that you'll have at least one discussion while you're on holiday about whether the arrival of tourism in Turkey is a good or a bad thing. For the record, like all of us who for most of the year have to cope with hectic schedules, with timetables, traffic and television, I can regret with a lot of sentiment the gradual disappearance in places – for ever – of what appears to be the idyllic, picturesque peasant life.

From what little I know of the traditional Turkish way of life, we might seriously mourn the possible passing of *some* of the honest, age-old family ideals that include, for example, open, unquestioning hospitality to all comers. But who am I to say that the fisherman shouldn't drop his nets and instead pick up boatloads of paying tourists, or that his daughter shouldn't learn English – and with it independence – and forsake her flowery pantaloons for a miniskirt?

You might have heard the one about the ideal tourist. The ideal tourist hands over the money and stays at home. Yes, after a glass or five of that cheap red wine, I've also sometimes wished that I could have kept Bodrum and Fethiye and numerous other tiny bays all to myself. But mass tourism *has* come to the coasts of Turkey and with it the benefits of cheap charter flights, more appealing hotels, easier shopping and fewer communication problems. I remember one hip Turk – a university graduate and now the owner of a bar and thirty bed and breakfast rooms – telling me how he regretted the commercialisation of "his" beaches but how pleased he is to see so many holidaymakers visiting his home patch. "It's not just the money," he said. "We Turks don't have a good image abroad. Now thousands of you can have a good relaxing holiday *and* learn that maybe these Barbaric Infidels are not so bad after all."

Turkey still has a desperately poor human rights record. Talk to Amnesty International if you want to know more about its shameful reputation. Or read *Midnight Express* for one account of life on the wrong side of the law in the Seventies.

Stresses and strains
It's also not possible to push an extra half a million people into a handful of seaside towns without the strain showing. Feeble electricity and sewage systems can collapse. Holiday accommodation can get thrown up with little thought for quality or reliability. One or two of the less attractive places become faceless holiday resorts which just offer beds, beach and sun. The food and the nightlife becomes international

Sightseeing at the Dolmabahçe Palace. Note the plastic bottle of mineral water. No serious tourist is ever without one.

and characterless, until only the contrived belly dancing evenings remind you you're in Asia. Mind you, I don't know of a Turkish bar selling English beer and no Turk has yet tried to master bingo.

Take a holiday in Turkey as soon as you can. And in the years to come, when the resort roads have been paved smooth, the hotel cooks have mastered fried egg and even bacon and there are air-conditioned supermarkets with Muzak, trolleys and Kelloggs cereals, you'll have the pleasure of sitting with the older Turks in some newly pedestrianised square by the mosque and reminiscing about the old days when you discovered the "real" Turkey.

The British are coming

Smallish specialist companies have been selling summer holidays to Turkey for some years. David Bennett, of the established small specialist Turkish Delight Holidays, first visited Turkey in November 1984. "I flew to Izmir and drove to Antalya and I was amazed at the sheer size and expanse of the place. It's also so beautiful and I really felt I'd found a place where time had stood still." His first brochure came out at the beginning of 1985. It featured Bodrum, Ölü Deniz and Kaş, and 354 intrepid travellers bought holidays from him that year. Five years on, the numbers are up to 7,000 and his biggest concern is finding places to feature "away from the masses".

Sunmed was one of the first companies to organise charter flights into Turkey offering holidays for large numbers of Britons. Sunmed's boss Vic Fatah had been selling holidays to Greece and the Greek islands for twelve years when he decided that "my next Greek island is the coast of Turkey".

In April 1985 he flew to Adana in the South near the Syrian border. "In six days I drove 2,600 kilometres. I drove West along the South coast, through cotton and tobacco country, looking for places I could feature in a brochure. Somehow nowhere felt cosy enough. Eventually I hit Alanya, Antalya and Side, which were then geared up for German visitors. At Ölü Deniz I found the perfect beach –

and not much else. Içmeler didn't exist. Bodrum reminded me of Mykonos. Even back then there were bars and disco music and flashing sunglasses. In those days Gumbet was a scrappy place. I knew I'd found resorts I could put in a brochure but somehow nothing that felt 100 per cent right. Then on the last day I drove into Altinkum. The feel of the place was right. The accommodation was there. And then I knew Turkey was the right place to be."

Altinkum is still Sunmed's best-selling resort; Vic Fatah reckons the next near-perfect resort for him is Patara.

Turkish discovery
"Spain was created by the mega tour operators.
Greece was created by the small holiday companies.
Turkey was created by journalists."

In 1986 newspapers started carrying some glowing articles by various travelling writers on "undiscovered" Turkey. This, Vic reckons, caused enough interest to make his first Go Turkey brochure a success. He'd counted on taking 4,000 people to Turkey that summer on the night charter flights he organised. (Flights to Turkey cost more than flights to Greece. He persuaded the charter companies to sell him night flights to Turkey at the same price as day flights to Greece.) By that October he'd sold 9,000 holidays.

In 1988, by the end of August the British holiday companies between them sent 325,666 holidaymakers to Turkey. For summer 1989 maybe up to half a million of us will fly over for a taste of Turkey.

And the 1990s? You can bet that as you read this there are tour operators driving up and down the coast roads of Turkey, trying to discover "new" resorts to feature and hunting for empty scraps of land to develop in the established places.

CHAPTER TWO:
CHOOSING THE RIGHT HOLIDAY

We dream and scheme all year to choose where we want to go and to raise the cash for a holiday – it's all part of the holiday experience. So it's desperately sad that some people end up not enjoying their precious weeks away one hundred and twenty per cent. I don't mean that they suffer some inexcusable holiday drama (for those sagas and what to do about them, read chapter fifteen). No, they've simply chosen the wrong holiday.

It's easily done. Some people, for example, might insist they want to do absolutely nothing all day but roast on a beach. But they forget to mention that they like their beaches fully equipped with sun beds, umbrellas and pedalos, not to mention readily available drinks and snacks and shops to potter round when the heat gets too much. A sugar-white beach that's completely empty and miles from civilisation might be paradise for one person – but holiday hell for another.

Whenever you're thinking of trying somewhere new for a holiday, make a list, in order of importance, of the things you really want from your trip.

- Do you enjoy meeting like-minded British people or would you be happy if you didn't hear another British voice for two weeks?
- Are you fussy about where you sleep or are you delighted to manage without coat-hangers and baths for a fortnight because a holiday bedroom is just for crashing out in at the end of the day?

- Do you like to dress up a little at night or are you happy to stuff three beach outfits and one cover-up in your case and live in them until you land back in Britain?
- Are you interested in seeing as many antiquities as you can and discovering the local art and culture, or are you content to have one or two ruins nearby so you can pop over for a quick spin round between the sunbathing?
- Do you like really getting to know the local people and their way of life, or do you prefer maybe to sample just one organised "Turkish evening" and bop till you drop every other night?

The problem of finding the right holiday is especially difficult when you're talking Turkey. Many travel agents have never been to Turkey themselves, so they can only rely on the sales talk in the brochures and what the tour operators tell them. Resorts are changing so fast that even those of us who know the coast have to be very careful to offer up-to-date information. And much of it is impossible to obtain because there is so much building work going on during every winter and (regrettably) during the summer months too. No-one knows in advance just how some resorts are going to cope with all the coachloads of extra tourists that will be pouring in. Last summer's favourite lazy *locanta* could just be this summer's noisiest nightspot.

Finally, the large mass-market travel operators have discovered Turkey. This isn't all bad news. They have the buying clout – if they choose to use it – to organise lower air fares, pay lower accommodation rates and demand higher hotel standards. But Turkey isn't Spain, or even another Greece. Filling brochures with words and pictures that suggest that might sell more holidays – but just who is going to buy them? Not everyone wants the very special qualities unique to Turkey.

To avoid making a mistake that you'll regret for the rest of the year, you should ask yourself what sort of holiday you really want – then, if you're sure it's Turkey, this book will help to point you towards the right resort.

Counting the cost
When you're budgeting for your holiday, don't forget to add in all the extras. Does the holiday company reserve the right to add late surcharges? How much will it cost you to get to the airport? How much is holiday insurance? Don't forget pocket money. It's true that the cost of living is wonderfully low in Turkey. But food, drink, transport and silk carpets don't come free – and remember that many travellers find that the shopping in Turkey is the most tempting of any country outside the Far East. In a nutshell: try to work out in advance what the whole holiday will cost you. Everything. The lot.

The journey
Think about the implications of a night flight. They're fine for saving money and precious holiday days but they're pretty exhausting. I don't recommend going to work the morning you land home! Remember too that you might have to leave your holiday rooms many hours before the flight leaves – that last day can be hell if you have young children in tow.

Consider the transfer times from the airport to your resort. You may feel happy that you can handle a four-hour flight, but then you sometimes have to add on a three-hour drive over mediocre roads. The journey can be far more gruelling that just flipping over to Benidorm, so be prepared.

Weather or not
Consider too the heat! The charts on page 22 give you some idea of Turkey's temperatures. The August sun can be cripplingly hot. If you're not tied to work or school holiday dates you might like to consider visiting Turkey outside July and August. Prices outside peak summer dates are lower, and the climate is easier to cope with. Holidays to Turkey in September are very popular: it's not always easy buying a last-minute flight in September.

The beer moves in for the tourist. A local resident remains unmoved.

If you'll be wielding a pushchair or perhaps a walking stick, beware the unmade roads and rough paths, the steep steps and tracks between beaches and accommodation. Point out your problem to the tour operator before you book and ask them to recommend suitable accommodation (if they can find any!). Make sure you have their assurances in writing. The travel agents Hogg Robinson publish a Recommended Resort and Hotel Guide, and very useful it is too. You can consult it for free at any branch of the Hogg Robinson chain.

Turks take holidays too!

Check out the dates of the Turkish religious festivals and national holidays. (They're listed on page 23.) If you really don't like crowds, these are the times to avoid. The beaches, the roads and the plumbing systems at the resorts are under the most stress during these periods.

Value for money

When you've got a pretty firm idea of the sort of holiday you want, and how much you can afford to pay for it, you'll find that – as with many buys in life – it can pay to shop around. Make the effort to find the small companies' brochures – their addresses are in this book – as well as asking at all your local travel agents about what's available from the bigger companies. It pays to do your homework.

When to go

The tour operators mainly offer holidays on the coast between April and October. The Black Sea coast has the mildest summer weather and the highest likelihood of summer rain and clouds. That's the price you pay for lush, green countryside.

The Aegean Coast is warmer than the Black Sea coast but cooler than the Mediterranean coast. Along the South coast, May, June, September and October are lovely months for hot sunshine with bright cloudless days from June to September and often longer.

Beware: the following temperature chart can be deceptive. The July and August temperatures can feel a lot hotter especially around midday.

	Jan	Feb	Mar	Apr	May	Jun	Jul	Aug	Sep	Oct	Nov	Dec
Marmara Region	**6**	**6**	**7**	**12**	**17**	**21**	**24**	**24**	**20**	**16**	**12**	**8**
(Istanbul)	43	43	45	54	63	70	75	75	68	61	54	47
Aegean Region	**9**	**10**	**12**	**16**	**21**	**25**	**28**	**28**	**24**	**19**	**15**	**11**
(Izmir)	48	50	54	61	70	77	82	82	75	66	59	52
Mediterranean	**11**	**12**	**13**	**17**	**21**	**23**	**29**	**29**	**25**	**21**	**16**	**12**
(Antalya)	52	54	56	63	70	77	84	84	77	70	61	54
Black Sea Region	**8**	**8**	**9**	**12**	**16**	**20**	**23**	**24**	**20**	**17**	**14**	**10**
(Trabzon)	47	47	48	54	61	68	73	75	68	63	57	50

Note: Centigrade temperature in **bold**. Fahrenheit in normal type.

Istanbul is really an all-year-round destination but in winter it can be bitingly cold and wet. In one week in November I've sat outside soaking up the sun on my face and, two days later, watched snowflakes try and settle on St Sophia. In the summer the city gets very hot and dry.

TURKISH PUBLIC HOLIDAYS

Religious Holidays

These dates change by around ten days each year.

1989

The feast of Ramazan (also known as the Sugar Festival – Şeker)	6, 7 & 8 May
The feast of Sacrifice – Kurban Bayram	13, 14, 15 & 16 July

Official Holidays

New Year's Day	1 January
National Sovereignty and Children's Day	23 April
Atatürk's Commemoration and Youth and Sports Day	19 May
Victory Day	30 August
Republic Day	28 October (half day)
	29 October (full day)

CHAPTER THREE:
WHAT TO TAKE WITH YOU

If you're worrying about packing a lounge suit or a ball gown, you've bought the wrong holiday. Casual dress is fine for all the coastal resorts, the restaurants and the excursions. So far, only the more cosmopolitan built-up places like Bodrum and Marmaris offer a selection of places where you can dress up at night. Even then, there's no need for formal wear – and they can be pretty dusty anyway. You'll be bringing home plenty of dust clinging to your shoes and best whites.

You can spot the old Turkey hands on a charter flight from Britain. They're the ones who travel light, with the minimum amount of luggage. What they do carry is mainly toiletries and medicines, suntan creams, paperbacks and a snorkel and flippers.

Pharmaceuticals

Raid your local chemists before you leave the country. You'll find that many of the everyday "necessities" we take for granted are hard to come by in all but the largest towns and cities. For holidays in "basic" accommodation, and for excursions, you'll want to travel with your own loo roll or paper tissues. If you're sensitive to smells, you might like to pack an air freshener for your shower room. The combination of heat and Turkish plumbing can be overwhelming.

Never underestimate the strength of the sun in Turkey. You can usually find the international brands of suntan oils and creams but it's wise to take with you your tried and tested favourites, and creams with a high factor number. The same applies for aftersun moisturisers and creams.

It's best to take an appropriate supply of toothpaste, shaving gear, tampons and condoms, rather than relying on local stocks. I remember looking for toothpaste in a well-stocked supermarket in a busy town. The shy girl at the check-out kept shaking her head and rubbing her chin. Then she giggled a lot but she still didn't want to sell me the packet of Gibbs I'd picked up. Another assistant joined in the arm-waving, and finally a third one had a brainwave and went through a mime of cleaning her teeth. "Yes, yes – that's it!" I said. Collapse of all parties in laughter. A different tube in a packet was produced, similar to the one I'd picked up but this one had a tell-tale picture of a mouth on it. I'd been trying to buy shaving cream.

Anti-bugging devices
Take some sort of insect repellant. You might be lucky and breeze through your trip without so much as a gnat-bite. You might not. You can buy various repellants in Britain which you rub or spray onto your skin to repel nasties. To keep unwelcome flying visitors out of your room you can invest in one of those lightweight plastic anti-mosquito devices that you plug into the electricity socket and feed with a fresh pellet every night. Buy them in Britain for around £6; you can buy refills for future trips.

Dry up
In many of the basic holiday hotels, the towels provided are so small you're likely to confuse them with face flannels. Take your own towels, for the room as well as the beach.

Plug it
I don't know whether it's to do with penny-pinching or a Muslim belief that you should always wash in running water, but many wash-basins don't have plugs. Take one of those

flat ones that covers any size hole. (Tip for sporty types: if you can't find one in the shops at home, a squash ball will plug the gap.)

Prepared for pictures
Take plenty of film for your camera with you. Even when you see film in Turkish shops, you might find that its sell-by date has long gone or that it's been stored in the searing heat, which can affect the pictures you take. Needless to say, you won't have much luck searching for tapes for a video camera. Take as many as you'll need.

Covering up
If you're planning to look into a mosque, you shouldn't show too much bare flesh. Women should carry a large lightweight scarf, to cover bare shoulders and/or legs. Men in short shorts and bare chests will need a cover-up too.

When the heat's on
Take a hat to protect yourself from the fierce midsummer sun. You'll be especially glad of it when you're wandering around the ancient ruins. Wafting the air with a Chinese-style paper fan you just happen to have in your pocket can help cool the situation a little.

Read all about it
Good local maps are hard to come by. If you're planning to branch off on your own with a hire car and explore the magnificent countryside, it's definitely a good idea to track down a map from a specialist shop in Britain.

You can buy books in Turkey about the archaeological sites, but the printing quality and their translation into English can leave a lot to the imagination. Buy your general guide books for serious archaeological and historical background reading in Britain. There's not a wonderful choice of holiday paperbacks in the Turkish shops. Buy before you leave home and when you run out, swap.

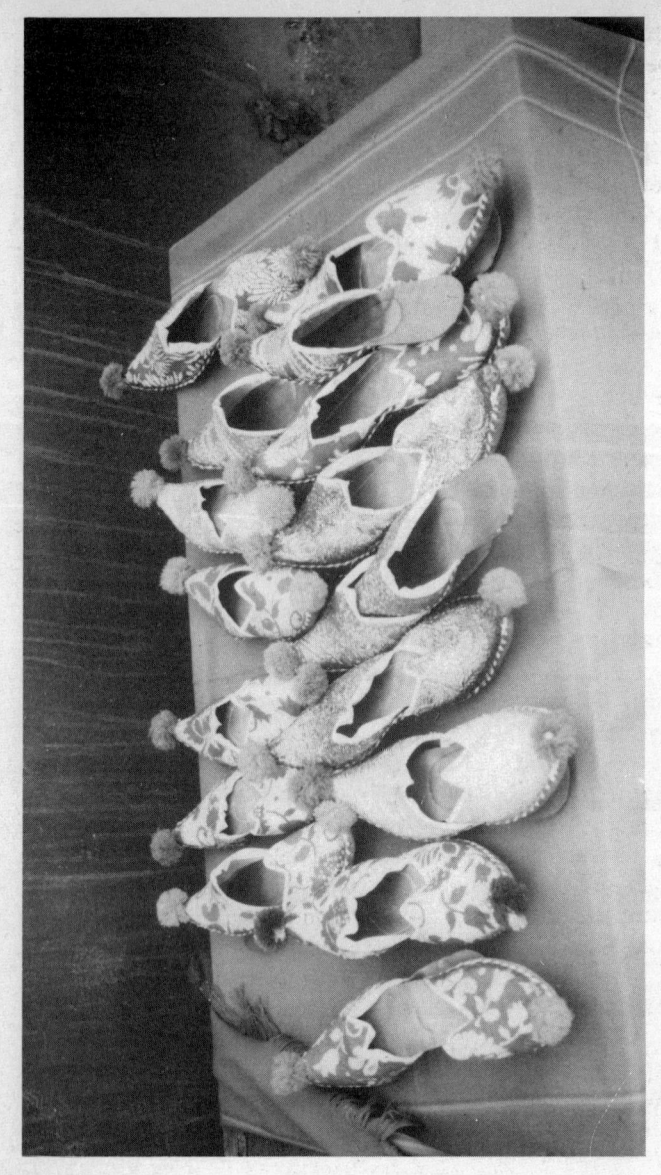

No need to pack bedroom slippers. There'll be plenty to choose from when you get there.

Feet first
Take comfortable, firm and flat shoes for scrambling round the historical sites. The streets can be obstacle courses, too, and as for pavements – what pavements? Plastic shoes for swimming off rocks are a sensible idea, and are especially useful on some beaches where sea urchins lurk under the water. Stepping on one can be very painful. You'll need to put antiseptic cream on the wound. The locals advise olive oil, which is supposed to help the spine slip out more easily. In emergencies use toothpaste as an antiseptic. Yoghurt, by the way, makes a soothing balm for sunburn.

Be a bag person
Show me an experienced traveller and I'll show you someone who knows the value of plastic bags. They're invaluable for wrapping breakable bottles, greasy tubes of suntan cream, collapsable cartons of Turkish Delight, soggy togs from a last-minute swim, dusty or sandy shoes. Take a good handful with you.

Beat the blackout
If you're staying in a small, newish resort, pack a torch. Street lighting is not top of the priority list for a newly developing Turkish town.

Favourite music
It can be worth taking some favourite tapes even if you're not packing a personal stereo. The tapes played on some boats and in the smaller bars can leave a lot to be desired. Boatmen and barmen are often only too happy to hear your choice of sounds.

Just in case
Travel with your travel documents, insurance papers, currency and any medicines you must take regularly, with you in your hand luggage just in case your suitcase is mislaid on the journey.

CHAPTER FOUR:
ESSENTIAL INFORMATION

Passport and visa
You can travel to Turkey for a holiday on a valid ten-year British passport or a British Visitor's one-year passport. If you're carrying a British passport you don't need a visa for stays of up to three months.

Travel insurance
You're not obliged to buy the insurance policy that your tour operator sells. But travelling without any policy at all is foolish. Check that the one you do buy has an emergency telephone number that is manned twenty-four hours a day. Check too that it covers you for air ambulance transport home if – heaven forbid – you should need it. And make sure that the maximum cover for the loss or theft of any one item is enough to cover your camera and possibly any valuable piece of jewellery – although Turkey is hardly a country that demands you pack the family heirlooms.

Holiday money
The Turkish unit of currency is the Lire. (In fact there are 100 *kurus* to a lire but you don't need to worry about them as inflation is rocketing away – last summer it was up to 45 per cent – and the *kurus* are never mentioned now.)

It's not worth buying Turkish lire in Britain. You get a better rate in Turkey and you can change traveller's cheques and sterling at the airports, whatever unearthly hour you land.

Most banks are open Monday to Friday from 8.30 am to noon and from 1.30 pm to five in the afternoon. They're closed on Saturdays, Sundays and public holidays. You'll need your passport to change money and sometimes you need it to change sterling. (The Turks sometimes won't recognise Irish and Scottish pound notes.) Banks all offer similar rates and often the exchange rate at the bank and the airport is the same as the rate offered by the hotels that change money (not all of them do). When you visit a bank to change money, be prepared for queues and much shuffling of paperwork.

Keep the receipts you're given when you change money. You might need to show them if you change any notes back into sterling as you leave the country. I'm told there is still a black market for currency deals. It is illegal and if by chance you're offered a street deal, you've no comeback if it goes wrong.

You can change Eurocheques for cash in a bank but they charge commission. You can use credit cards in the larger top hotels in Istanbul but in restaurants you'll need cash. Some carpet and leather shops now take credit cards but you've less chance of a discount if you use one. Sometimes the agreed price goes up when you insist on paying with plastic. Many hotels use a bead system. You buy the beads in reception and use them to pay for drinks and so on in the hotel.

Tipping tips

In Turkey you don't have to put up with hotel staff, waiters and taxi drivers always hanging around in an obvious way waiting for a tip. Service is generally included in the bill at restaurants. A little extra for the friendly service you'll be getting is always appreciated. Taxi drivers don't expect a tip but it's easy to round up the price to the nearest hundred.

Last summer I stayed for a week in a top hotel in Istanbul. Each night a gentle elderly man would turn down the bed, change the towels, tidy up and leave a little box of Turkish Delight. (It was indeed a luxury hotel.) I looked out for him before I checked out and gave him about £4 as a tip, which is considered very little by the Americans-in-Europe standard. He came rushing after me as I was leaving and to show his gratitude pressed armsful of the hotel's free soaps, flannels, shampoos and Turkish Delight on me. As I said, the Turkish don't take tips for granted.

Telephones

You want to phone home? Some hotels, especially in Istanbul, have international dialling – but they often charge a hefty commission for the privilege. To save money, you're better off in a public call box. Actually, they don't take money but tokens called *büyük jeton*, which you buy from a PTT (post) office. You need to buy a good handful of the largest tokens, which cost 375 TL each (summer 1988 prices) and give you about 20 seconds on a call to Britain on the new automatic system. You also need a lot of determination and patience.

An automatic push-button call box labelled *Milletlerarasi* takes international calls. If the red light under the push buttons is lit it means the box is out of order. If it isn't lit, it means either that the box is working or that the red light is out of order. Pick up the receiver. Put in one token in the slot at the top. When the red light to the right of the pictorial instructions goes out, press 9. It is often engaged. When it isn't, you hear a new dial tone. Press 44 for the UK. Then dial your home STD code minus the first 0, then the number. If the red light goes on while you're connected, or if you hear a chime on the line, put more tokens in immediately. It's sometimes easier to get through after about 8pm Turkish time.

Current affairs

Turkey runs on 220-volt AC current and uses Continental-style two-pin plugs. Take an adaptor with you. If you forget, you might just find an electrician who can fit a local plug for you.

Turkey is still coming to terms with twentieth-century technology: it's easy to see why phone calls don't always get through first time.

Topless tans
Nudity is illegal in this Moslem country. However outbreaks of female topless sunbathing do occur on the popular beaches and round hotel pools. Common sense should tell you when it's OK. The locals will soon let you know when it isn't.

Drugs
Even the smallest drug offences are punishable by severe prison sentences. If you're not convinced, read *Midnight Express* by Billy Hayes with William Hoffer (published by Abacus at £3.99).

Imports
If you can't enjoy a holiday without your favourite brand of spirit and/or tobacco, Turkish customs allow you to take into the country tax-free: seven (70cl) bottles of spirit, of which no more than three shall be the same brand, and 400 cigarettes or 50 cigars or 200 grams of tobacco. Istanbul airport sensibly has a duty-free shop open to passengers *arriving* in Turkey. The choice isn't as wide as in British airports but the basic duty-free and tax-free lines are covered.

The hotels in established places are used to visitors who can't face Turkish tea or Turkish coffee in the morning and want "ordinary" coffee. They sell cups of instant coffee – known as "Nes", whatever the brand – as extras and they don't usually provide free hot water for those with their own jar. Instant coffee is very expensive in Turkey and for places where you can get hot water you might like to know that the government allows you to import 1.5kg of instant coffee without paying duty at customs.

For the rules on what you can take home duty and tax free, see chapter seven on shopping.

Accommodation
Holiday accommodation by the Turkish seaside runs from small wooden huts in camp sites described by the press and

The sign might be tatty, the accommodation can be pretty basic but 'VIP' is rarely an overstatement for service.

holidaymakers as hen coops, potting sheds, dog kennels and wendy houses and by some brochures as chalets, right through to international, sophisticated and spanking-new hotels with pools, bars and laser-show nightclubs. Somewhere in the middle are charming family hotels, tatty old-fashioned hotels, plain and basic rooms next to a delightful family house and plain and basic rooms in dreary, badly-built blocks.

Taste and price obviously dictate what sort of bed and surroundings you choose for your holiday. A lot of hotels are registered with the Ministry of Culture and Tourism, which means they have to offer certain facilities. The top classification is Luxury, then there are four grades from First down to Fourth.

A *Pansiyon* probably offers the most authentic brush with Turkish life. A pansiyon (the brochures nearly all translate this to "pension", though one or two lyrically upgrade it to "villa") can be a room in a family house or a purpose-built block of rooms with few frills, usually looked after by a family. There may or may not be a restaurant (*lokanta*) attached. Don't expect your landlord or landlady to necessarily speak English. These and village rooms are nearly always very simply furnished. Be pleased if yours has coat-hangers and a shower curtain. Such rooms are rarely a shock to anyone who has used taverna accommodation and village rooms in Greece. The "ensuite" comprises a loo, shower and washbasin. There won't be any cooking facilities but with so many cheap eating-places you wouldn't ever want them.

Hotel accommodation varies a lot. Price is one reasonable guide and the age of a place is another. The older places are often not built with Europeans in mind. Some of the brand-new places have been/are being built to orders from the tour operators who know what their customers will and will not put up with. Read through a few brochures to get the hang of how the different holiday companies describe the same set of rooms or hotel.

CHAPTER FIVE: HOLIDAY HEALTH

Jabs

You don't need any compulsory inoculations before you visit Turkey. However, the latest advice from the DHSS recommends typhoid and cholera jabs and immunisation against polio. The DHSS booklet *Traveller's Guide to Health* (February 1988) also mentions taking precautions against malaria but this is not necessary for holidays on the Aegean and Mediterranean coastline, or for Istanbul and the Black Sea holiday resorts.

There was an outbreak of hepatitis on the coast at the end of the 1988 season, and a gamma-globulin jab against hepatitis is strongly recommended. This injection should be taken just a few days before departure. Immunity then normally lasts for three months.

While you're being done for this lot, you might also choose to have a course of vaccinations against tetanus. Then if you suffer a dubious gash you won't need a local anti-tetanus jab. These days, in many places in the world it's wise to avoid needles whenever you can. Consult your doctor or an immunisation centre at least two months before your holiday because for maximum protection you need two typhoid injections four to six weeks apart.

Of course, if there's any drug or medication that you need for a particular medical condition, make sure you have a more than adequate supply before you leave home.

The Turkey trots
On Turkish holidays you sometimes get to know about your fellow guests' digestive systems before you know their names. The heat, the water, the unusual foods, the occasional local rough-and-ready hygiene can all have an effect. Most people have a "favourite" remedy for coping with diarrhoea. (Mine's Imodium, available from most chemists in Britain.) Buy yours before you leave home.

If you do succumb on holiday, conventional wisdom advises that you drink plenty of liquid (not alcohol or strong coffee). Eat very little for the first twenty-four hours and then common sense and your body's instincts will probably point you towards plain, bland food such as bread, boiled eggs and boiled rice.

Beware of dehydration which can follow a prolonged period of sickness and vomiting. It's a very serious condition and must be given full medical attention. Women using the contraceptive pill must remember that vomiting can negate the pill's effect.

Water wisdom
Follow the local advice on whether the water is drinkable. In Istanbul, for example, the water is so heavily chlorinated it's safe to drink – but not exactly tasty. If in doubt, don't drink the tap water and don't take ice in your drinks. Spring water in plastic bottles is cheap and easily available. You usually end up carrying a bottle everywhere with you for a cooling swig whenever the heat gets to you. After a day or two in Turkey, you begin to feel naked without your bottled water and your loo roll in your beach bag.

Beware of the sun
Writing this section on a damp drizzly day in London makes it difficult to remember that you can suffer from too much sun in Turkey. But believe me, you can – and if you do, you'll lose precious days of your holiday trying to recover. Take strong suntan creams with you and use them. The more fair-skinned and unused to the sun you are, the higher

the degree of protection you need. Re-apply creams and oils after you've been swimming.

One of the easiest ways to burn badly is to take to the sea. The cooling breezes mask the harm that the sun is doing, but the rays can reach you even through sea water. Snorkeling is a common way of burning your back, so it's a good idea to wear a T-shirt in the sea. The other horribly common way to burn badly is to fall asleep in the sun. A morning glass or two of *raki* can act as a strong sleeping pill. If you do burn you can try cooling the skin with yoghurt.

Too much unaccustomed hot sun can cause you to develop a high temperature, feel ill and maybe sweat and even vomit. Then you need to drink a lot of water – but not too quickly – cool yourself with damp flannels and take some Aspirin to lower your temperature. You should do all this in a cool, dark room, and rest. Serious heatstroke is dangerous but rare.

Once bitten . . .

A knowledgeable tour rep confidently recommends rubbing jellyfish stings with diluted ammonia. You find diluted ammonia in urine. I suppose it depends on how desperate you are. Scratching a mosquito bite can cause a scar. Lemon juice or that ammonia again might relieve the bites. Better still are the products you can buy in British chemists to relieve the swelling and the itching.

Beware of sea urchins under the waves along some stretches of the coast. If you step on one, the spine is not poisonous but it's painful to remove. Baby lotion, olive oil or whatever cream or oil you have to hand might help the spine work its way out.

Mosquitos are at their most active between dusk and around midnight. If you're a prime target for the pests (and there seems to be no known reason why the monsters feast off some of us and ignore others) you'll need to cover your exposed flesh when the sun goes down. British chemists stock a fair choice of strong repellants you can rub over your skin. Again, buy before you travel.

Well it probably can't do you any harm . . .

If you're travelling on a night flight have your insect repellant in your hand luggage. You'll need it at the airport. A mosquito killing device you can plug into the mains in your room is worth buying. They cost around £6 in Britain. You need to remember to plug yours in with a fresh "tablet" at dusk.

For your convenience
If you're staying in a newly-built hotel in an established resort, toilets shouldn't be a worry. However, in old cafes and restaurants, be prepared for encounters with the old-style no-seat "elephant's feet" lavatory. It's the mark of the experienced lady traveller to come out of one with unsplashed feet. When you're squatting, watch your trouser pockets. You can lose a lot of loose change this way. Stand back when you pull the chain – the jets can be fierce. Take your own paper. Much of the Turkish plumbing can't cope with paper down the pan, whatever style the loo. There'll be a basket nearby for used loo paper. If you've ever had a holiday in Greece, you'll know the form.

CHAPTER SIX:
GETTING AROUND

Tour operators offer excursions to the worthwhile sights around the area you're staying in. You should reckon on paying around £20 for a day trip. Excursions are usually priced in pounds sterling and you can pay for them with traveller's cheques or cash. (See chapter eleven for information on the sights that are worth seeing.) You may want to strike out on your own, just for the adventure of it, or to give yourself a flexible itinerary. Getting around under your own steam is quite easy and not particularly hazardous, providing you know the rules and the local customs.

Car hire

To hire a car you need a current driving licence that you've held for at least one year. An international driving permit is not compulsory but Europcar say that one can be helpful if you are stopped by the police. As an example of prices, the Europcar Superdrive rate for March 1989 for a Renault 12 (type B car) is 413,000 Turkish Lire a week with unlimited mileage and including tax. Collision damage waiver costs 7000 TL a day plus 12% VAT and an optional personal accident insurance is 1500 TL a day. That all works out at 479,640 TL a week (£159.88 at an exchange rate of £1=TL 3000). Plus petrol, of course. To get Europcar's Superdrive rate, you have to book in Britain with at least 24 hours' notice, and you can pay for it in the UK or in Turkey.

   The major package holiday companies offer car hire which you book before you travel (although they can also

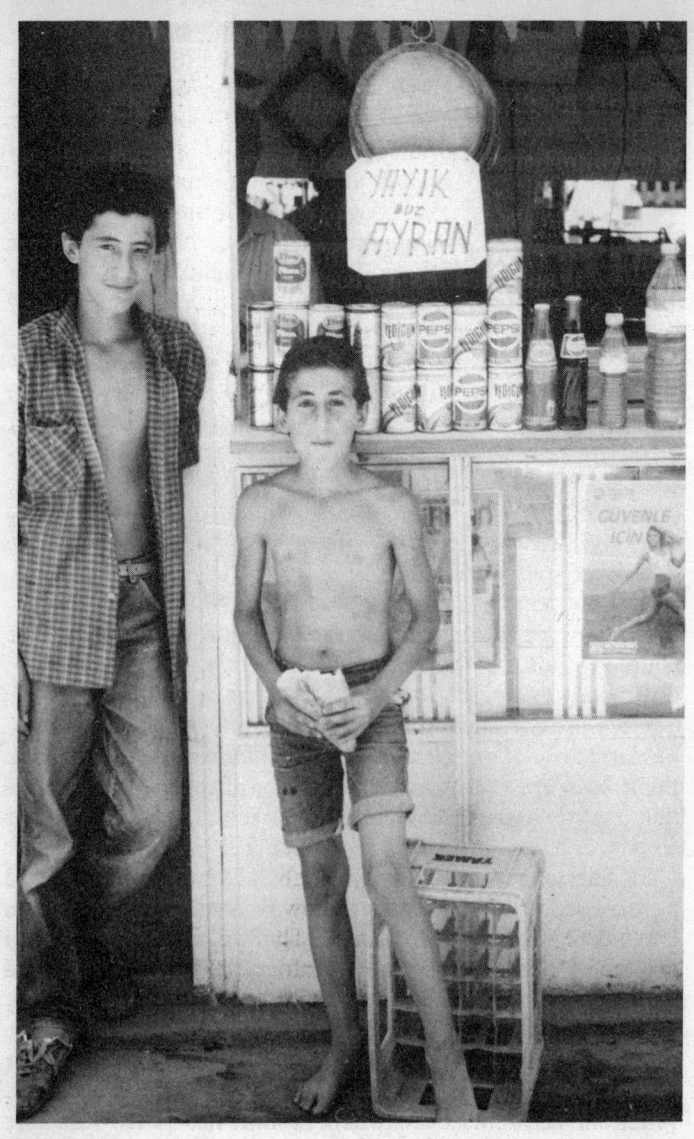

Open all hours for takeaway snacks and drinks.

sometimes arrange spur-of-the-moment car hire when you're in Turkey). Prices range from around £160 to £290 a week (depending on the month and the company) including collision damage waiver and local VAT, but not petrol or personal accident insurance. The minimum age for drivers is often 21, although Sunmed allow a minimum age of 19.

For driving the smallest engine cars – groups B, C, D and E – Europcar have a minimum age limit of 19, for the bigger (and more expensive) cars in groups F and I the minimum age is 24, and for the most powerful cars in groups G and H you need to be at least 27 years old.

Any second drivers should be named when you hire the car and must show their licence, otherwise the insurance is invalid. When you budget for a hire car, remember that often the Turkish tax (12%) and insurance, collison damage waiver and possibly a delivery fee will be added to the bill, plus of course the cost of the petrol you use – which in 1988 was around £1 a gallon.

On the road

The main roads are well maintained and signposted. The country roads are not: they can fizzle out into stony paths or dirt tracks. At night, the roads are rarely lit – and neither are the donkeys or the goats or even some other cars. Turkish drivers like their horns. On country roads they use them frequently, to warn that they're about to overtake or that they're coming round a bend. It's a sensible idea to copy.

In Turkey you drive on the right. There's a 50 kph (32 mph) speed limit in cities, towns and built-up areas. Elsewhere it's 90 kph (55 mph). The symbols on road signs are easily understood. They conform to the International Protocol on Road Signs. Historical sites are indicated by yellow signposts.

Any holidaymaker who drives in Istanbul is fearless or crazy. Turkey as a whole has a high road accident rate. After an accident, even when no-one has been hurt, the police have to be called and a report filed. I am forever

Everyone flocks to the barbers for a head massage as well as a haircut.

being told how, after an accident, local tempers get very frayed. Foreigners should keep cool and calm, and stay out of the fracas.

If your car breaks down, people can be generous with help. Once when I was travelling with a male colleague, the car ran out of water just outside Marmaris. (I don't think we'd screwed the radiator cap on properly and it was one of those dramatic steaming affairs.) The local restaurant manager came out with bottles of water, advice on what to do (communicated by extravagant mime) and muscle power to help push the thing off the road. Needless to say, no-one charged us a penny for their help.

On some coastal roads you might see the burliest juggernaut driver screech to a halt for no apparent reason. Look closer and you'll see he swerved to avoid some small rocks in the road. When he gets out and very gently lifts the "rocks" to the side of the road, you'll know he's helping to preserve Turkey's tortoise population.

Flying round Turkey
It's possible to catch an internal flight with Turkish Airlines (THY – *Turk Hava Yollari*). They have a network of flights to Istanbul from Dalaman, Izmir and Antalya. As an example of prices, the Dalaman-Istanbul return flight in summer 1988 was £80 if you paid for the flight in Britain, but less (around £65) if you paid in Turkey in Turkish Lire. The manager of THY in London tells me that it's possible to reserve seats in London before you travel and pay the lower price in Turkish Lire when you are in Turkey.

The flights are heavily booked around the Turkish holiday dates (see chapter two). In 1989, a pre-bookable two-night excursion to Istanbul, including bed and breakfast, cost between £135 and £145 (from Sunmed).

On the buses
There are buses in the cities, and they always seem to be full of people. You need to buy a ticket in advance from a ticket kiosk – they're not always easy to track down. You'll be

lucky to find a driver or fellow-passenger who can speak enough English to help you find your way, so it's a good way of getting hopelessly lost in a strange city. In any case, taxis are so cheap that they're a sensible alternative to the crush and confusion of the buses.

Long-distance buses do run from Istanbul to the Aegean and Mediterranean coasts, and between coastal towns, but the journeys take many hours. As an approximate guide, Istanbul to Antalya takes twelve hours. Dalaman to Bodrum should be three hours and Dalaman to Antalya eight hours. If you dislike cigarette smoke, you won't last the distance.

Value-added taxis

Taxis are a common and convenient way of getting around Istanbul and the resorts. The fares are low compared to British cabs – but then the cars aren't exactly in the same league. Your hotel or tour rep will know the average fare for a particular journey, which you can use as a guide when you use a taxi without a meter. Tipping isn't expected but most tourists round up the price to include a little over. In Istanbul, I've twice had a driver who didn't have enough change for a large note, while I didn't have enough small change for the fare. Both times the driver rounded the price *down* and took the lesser note.

Turkey with stuffing

The scruffy minibuses or large cars they call *dolmus* (DOLL-moosh) are cheap and useful. They usually gather at one central point in a town or village, or near a popular beach. When the *dolmus* is full it heads off on its route. There are no set stops and you can get off where you like or flag one down anywhere along the route. You pay the driver.

You should perhaps know that the word *dolmus* literally means "stuffed". They do certainly pack them in. In the larger towns a *dolmus* will have its final destination marked up in the front window.

Without a hitch
Seasoned Turkey travellers tell of problem-free hitch-hiking around the Western shores. But they are men. As a holidaymaker in a seaside resort or town, you should never need to hitch-hike and I certainly wouldn't risk recommending single women to try it – in Turkey or in Britain.

CHAPTER SEVEN: SHOPPING

At a British airport, you can usually tell which holidaymakers have just landed home from Turkey. They're the ones wearing squeaky-new leather jackets and carrying a bundle of carpet. Shopping in Turkey is brilliant. Even if you're staying in one of the remoter resorts, there's usually an excursion to a town where you can shop for a local rug, something in leather, plenty of cheap quirky souvenirs and boxes of filling, fattening Turkish Delight.

Bargain for bargains

If you hate haggling, you won't enjoy shopping in Turkey. The initial asking price always allows for some serious bargaining. For carpets, leather clothes and anything else of value, the custom is to start the negotiations with a glass of tea or a cold drink. Don't be embarrassed – it's free and it puts you under no obligation. This sort of shopping can't be done in a hurry, and the shopkeeper never appears to begrudge the time it can take before he clinches a deal. As you sip his tea and enjoy a long sit in the welcome coolness of his shop, it sometimes pays to tell him that you're really shopping around for the lowest price and you'll come back to him if his is the best offer. You may well find the price drops even more. He'll know the going rate of any item and what his competitors down the street will eventually offer.

Try never to have to buy anything in a hurry. Most people sensibly shop around in a lazy inquiring way at the beginning of their stay and firm up the final offers a day or so before they go home. Shopping at the end of your holiday will only be a mistake if you fall in love with one particular leather coat or jacket that doesn't fit you and there isn't time for the shopkeeper to have one in your size sent over from the factory.

The more things you buy from one shop, the bigger the "Special Price" or discount. Plenty of carpet and leather shops now take credit cards. If you pay cash in one of these, ask for a bigger discount. (If you spend hours agreeing a price and then produce some plastic, don't be surprised if the price goes straight up again.)

Rugs and carpets

The ultimate Turkish souvenir. Even if you have absolutely no intention of buying, it's worth visiting a shop or two to see the designs and colours and to experience the laid-back but oh so serious Turkish sales talk. Buying a rug or carpet worth more than £20 is serious stuff, involving lots of tea-sipping and straight-faced haggling.

If you do plan to spend a lot of money on a rug, it'll pay you to do some homework first and to leave plenty of time for shopping for one. Many tour reps have worked out a private commission deal with a shop in the area – but that's not necessarily a con trick: you shouldn't automatically avoid any shop that's recommended to you.

Fun souvenirs

Cheaper souvenirs that you'll see around include embroidered Turkish slippers, fezzes – once the mark of a Sultan and banned for many years by Atatürk (I bet most of the ones bought turn up at fancy dress parties) – decorative kebab skewers (for fancy barbecues), sponges, nuts and Turkish Delight. Souvenir shops stock attractive and colourful ceramic plates, tiles, bowls, cups and so on. Cheap and cheerful.

Designer fakes

I thought Hong Kong had cornered the market in fake

designer sports shirts until I first went to Turkey. You want a crocodile on your chest? No problem. Take care washing these fakes. A hot wash and a tumble-dry can reduce a shirt by several sizes and the crocodile can sometimes shed tears of dye.

Jewellery

Jewellery lovers can have a field day. You'll find the biggest choice of shops selling the more expensive gold and gems in the Grand Bazaar at Istanbul.

Antiques

In Turkey it's not against the law to buy and sell Turkish antiques – but it is strictly illegal to export them. (If you visit certain museums round the world, especially in Britain, you'll soon realise why the Turks implemented this law: sadly too late to keep some of their finest treasures in the country.) However the "genuine antique" souvenirs you haggle for in a bazaar were aged well before they left the factory.

Meerschaum pipes

They're the pipes with the white bowls carved into fanciful figures like animals and old men's heads. Meerschaum is a delicate soft white stone and as the export of meerschaum blocks is now banned, the pipes are all hand-carved in Turkey. Pipe collectors will marvel both at the carvings and at the prices, which are a lot cheaper than you'd ever find in Britain.

"Eat sweet, speak sweet"

In a traditional Turkish home, visitors are greeted with lemon juice for scenting their hands. Then sweet treats are offered with the sentiment "Let us eat sweet and speak sweet", followed usually by thick rich coffee or maybe a plate of fruit. The sweet cakes and the *locum* which we know as Turkish Delight are so sugary, they go straight to your fillings. Every town has at least one cake shop where

You can buy a fez as a souvenir although strictly speaking they were banned by Atatürk, who founded the Turkish cloth cap industry at a stroke.

you can sip coffee and eat *baclava* and other syrupy-sweet pastries.

Turkish Delight is an obvious present to take home. One sweet-toothed holidaymaker I know brought back 25 kilos of the stuff. The best is desperately sweet and gooey – delicious. Buy it at a specialist shop if you can: the sweets will be fresher and you'll find more choice. Don't be embarrassed to ask for a taste. Some *locum* is made with nuts. If you see darker pieces rolled in coconut, they're made from carrot – but they're sweet and sticky too. Most shopkeepers will make up a mixed box for you. I've no idea how long it keeps before it tastes stale. In my house, a boxful disappears in two days.

Those blue shoe-boxes you see on the hills are beehives. If you visit a specialist honey shop you'll find several different varieties on sale, all with distinctive flavours. Traditionally, pine honey (*cam*) is eaten at breakfast to help digestion problems, and has slightly less sugar than thyme honey (*kekik*). Flower honey (*cicek*) is often given to children. You can also sometimes buy honeycombs. Wrap your honey well in plastic bags for the journey home. When a jar leaks in your case, it's not a pretty sight.

Green or red channel?

Turkey is a non-EEC country (but they're working on it) and therefore the regulations for what you can bring back into Britain without paying extra duty and tax are *currently* as follows:

- Alcohol
  1 litre of spirits plus 2 litres of wine
  OR 2 litres of fortified wine plus 2 litres of wine
  OR 4 litres of wine

- Tobacco
  200 cigarettes
  OR 100 cigarillos
  OR 50 cigars
  OR 250 grammes tobacco

- Perfume: 50 grammes or 2 fl oz
- Toilet water: 250 cc or 9 fl oz
- Other goods: up to £32-worth, including a maximum of 50 litres of beer and 25 lighters.

Beware the sales person or the rep who claims that you won't have to pay VAT or duty at customs. When you land back in Britain, if the value of goods you buy in Turkey (not including alcohol, tobacco and perfumes) comes to more than £32, you're supposed to go through the red channel and declare what you have bought. Customs officers at Gatwick, by the way, have been on a course to learn about Turkish carpets. They are also aware that carpet shops offer receipts to show at customs, stating less than the price you paid. The duty men are pretty clued-up on the real value of leather coats, too. It's not true that an opened bottle of booze or packet of cigarettes doesn't count in the tally. They do.

CHAPTER EIGHT: TASTING TURKEY

"First the eyes should be full and then the stomach" – Turkish proverb on the importance of making food look as good as it'll taste.

If you're interested in food, you'll find Turkish cooking a joy. Gourmets rate it up there alongside French and Chinese as the best in the world. If you've ever been stuck in a remote resort in Greece with meatballs, salad, stewed lamb and more meatballs, the Turkish cuisine could have you dancing in the streets.

You'll never find a tin-opener in a Turkish kitchen. You *will* find loads of whatever fresh local vegetables and fruits are in season, lots of meat (but no pork in this Moslem country) and plenty of fish. By the coast, the fish comes in off the boat in the morning and it can be on the grill and on your plate that night. Turkey is one of the few countries in the world that is self-sufficient in food. Not having to import costly foods helps explain why eating in Turkey costs so little. Instant coffee is one recognisable import you'll come across. It's brought in to make us tourists feel at home and can cost as much as £7 sterling a jar. Many of the famous and common dishes like charcoal-grilled skewered meats and döner kebabs were first dreamt up and perfected centuries ago by the Sultan's cooks in Istanbul's Topkapi Palace.

Restaurants in Turkey are casual and they're often open from morning until late at night. If there is a menu and someone has made an attempt to translate it into English, rest assured that the cooking will be better than the shaky translations. Among the oddities I've spotted on menus are "Gourd teacher fainted", "Priest fainted", "Ladies thighs" and "Wedding soap".

The form is to walk over to the chilled display cabinet and see what's on offer. Then you can order by pointing to what you want. There's no shame in visiting a restaurant to inspect the dishes on display and then leaving if they're not what you're after. Don't pre-judge a place by its decor. Some of the best banquets are to be had in rooms with peeling paint, wobbly tables and paper tablecloths. I've had some of the best meals of my life sitting at a trestle table in a field! Anyway, when you think how little you'll be paying for the meal, you can hardly demand pink linen and cut glass. Hospitality is an integral part of the Turkish culture. It's not uncommon for a waiter who hasn't got the dish you particularly want to run down the road to another restaurant and fetch one for you.

As everywhere in the world, except maybe at McDonald's, you'll find that the quality of dishes can vary from place to place. One chef's made-in-heaven, unforgettable *börek* can be another's duff rubber ball. Turkish food is served warm, not hot, the same as in Greece. That's nothing to do with slapdash service. It's how the Turks like their food.

Just for starters

The Turkish starters, *mezes*, are varied and filling enough to stand in as a full lunch. Some restaurants serve a special selection of mezes, with a taste of a few on one plate. The huge variety of mezes include melon, aubergines, stuffed peppers, vine leaves or aubergine, salads, fried mussels on a stick, hot flaky pastries filled with cheese and herbs, dishes of yoghurt with cucumber, mashed grilled aubergine and a creamy humus of blended and flavoured chick peas. And that's just for starters. By the way, the purple and black shiny skinned aubergines, which the Americans call eggplants, feature a lot in Turkish cooking. Someone, somewhere must be compiling "101 things a bright Turk can do with an aubergine".

And to follow . . .

If you can get past the mezes, you'll find sizzling meats and fish on offer.

The fish restaurants with the greatest choice are in Istanbul and along the nearby coast. Most restaurants selling fish along the Turkish coast will offer the catch of the day as a main course. You do need to check the price you'll be paying before you order. Some restaurants in the brasher resorts spot a tourist coming and hike up the final bill for the unpriced fish accordingly. If a restaurant isn't bursting at the seams with diners, it's even possible to haggle over the fish price before ordering and negotiate a lower one. In places that don't particularly specialise in fish you must judge the freshness of the catch in the chilled display cabinet.

When it comes to meat, you won't find pork in this Moslem country but there's no shortage of lamb and beef. The most known and exported meat dish is probably *şiş kebab* – chunks of meat threaded on a skewer and grilled over a charcoal fire. (In Dublin there are now Turkish takeaways called Abrakebabra!). DIY barbecue restaurants are fun. Each outdoor table has its own charcoal brazier. You order the meats and/or fish you fancy and cook them yourself. Follow your nose to find one.

Vegetarians in Turkey happily aren't reduced to omelettes and chips for every meal. There are many meatless and fishless dishes using the local vegetables and rice. Turkish *pilav* rice is especially good, and so are their cracked wheat pilaf dishes, *bulgur pilavi*. After most typical Turkish meals I find I'm hard pressed to manage even a slice of fruit for afters. But if you're up to a dessert, it'll be something sweet, sticky and probably nutty. Turkish cooks like their syrup and produce cakes and desserts so sweet they go straight to your fillings.

As with the other dishes, the afters will usually be on display in the chilled cabinet and you can point to the one

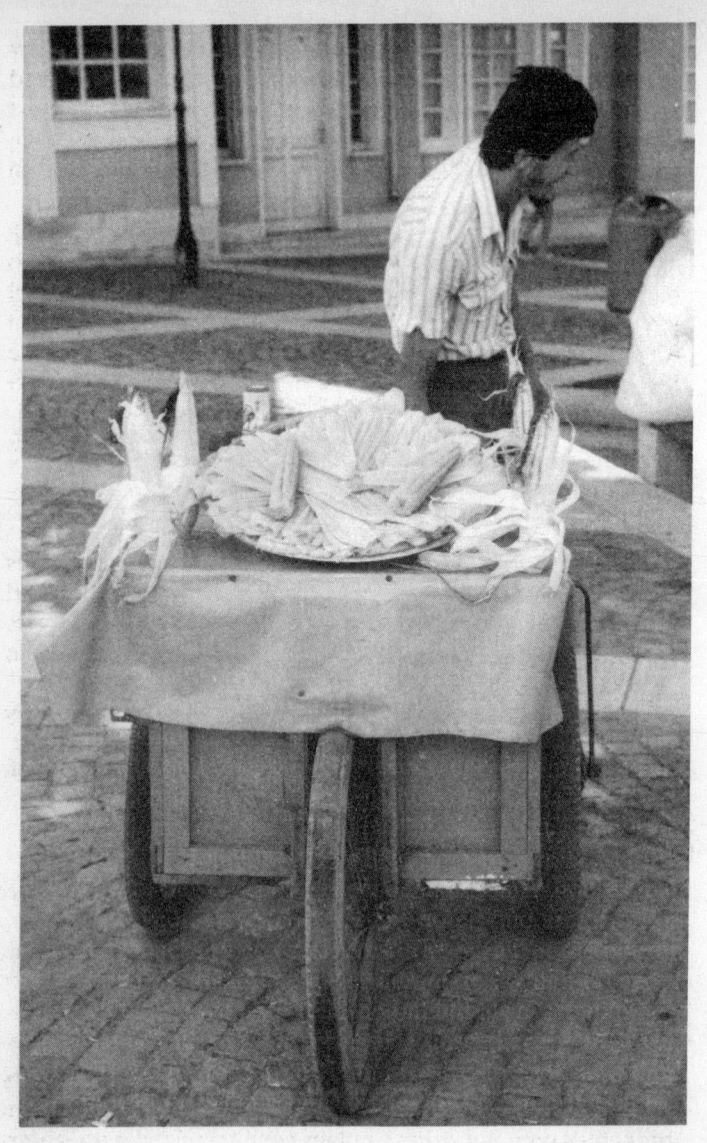

Meals on wheels: you don't have to travel far to find a snack.

that you fancy. If there's a menu, you'll find that the syrupy concoctions have delightful names like Lips of the Beloved and Lady's Navel (both fried treats) or Nightingale's Nest which is a pastry stuffed with nuts. If you've holidayed in Greece you'll recognise *baklava*, a nutty pastry swamped in syrup.

In the larger towns you'll find "pudding shops" selling milk puddings which the locals love. If you're old enough to be nostalgic for the hippy days of peace and love, in Istanbul the Pudding Shop with the bright orange front on the main road near St Sophia was *the* hippy meeting place in the Sixties. These days it's fun to spot the occasional and now respectable and near middle-aged tourists reliving their youth. The most famous dessert is, of course, Turkish Delight, *lokum*.

Tea, coffee and soft drinks

The Turkish drink their tea – and lots of it – in small glasses without milk but usually with a lot of sugar. Apple tea and mint tea are also popular and well worth trying. Hotels catering for Europeans now usually serve breakfast tea in cups with milk.

Turkish coffee is strong, well brewed and served in tiny cups without milk or cream. It's rarely served for breakfast. When you order a Turkish coffee you need to say how much sugar (*şekerli*) you want.

sade = without sugar
az = slightly sweetened
orta = medium sweet
çok = very sweet

When your coffee (*kahve*) is served, let the grounds settle to the bottom of the cup for a minute or so.

Water

Bottled Turkish mineral water is readily and cheaply available, fizzy or still. Check that the seal hasn't been broken. *Ayran* is a drink of plain yoghurt mixed with water. The quality varies from cafe to cafe. In areas where you've

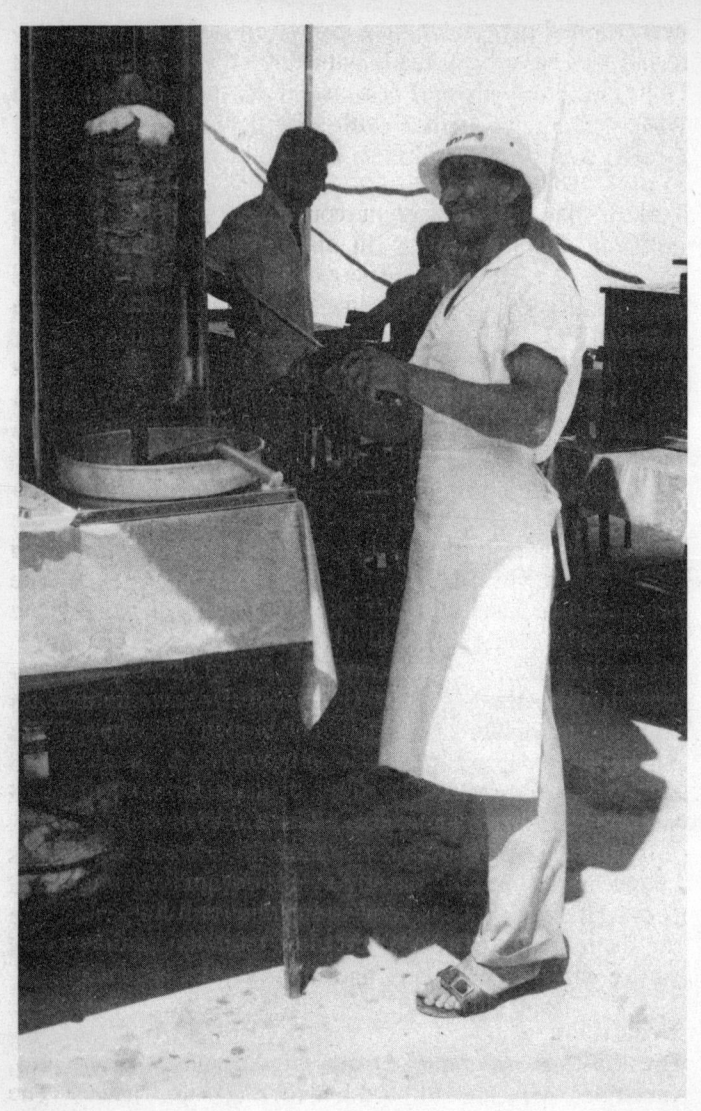

The döner kebab was first created in the Sultan's kitchens in Topkapi Palace, Istanbul.

been warned off drinking the tap water, beware the *ayran* – it may not have been made with bottled water. Cokes and Fantas are everywhere. For a change try the Turkish bottled black cherry juice. Mixed with soda it's called *vişne suyu*.

Wines and raki
Turkey may be a Moslem country but you'll have no problems finding alcohol. In many places the "wine list" reads just "red or white". There aren't many different labels and, as Turkish wine is not expensive, you can try a different bottle with every different meal to find your favourite. They don't go in for vintage wines – bottles come undated – so there's no need to bone up on the good and the bad years. Doluca and Kavaklidere are labels you're most likely to be offered. Most wines are dry – *sek*. There is locally made gin and vodka which are obviously cheaper than imported brands. In many bars, if you don't like the local stuff, you need to specify that you want imported spirits when you order a drink. (And vice versa in the sharper more European-type bars where the barman may be anxious to sell the higher priced drinks.)

You'll also find a range of sweet fruit liqueurs. If you want a Turkish brandy, opt for the more expensive brands (still much cheaper than any French brandy). Like me, you might find the cheapest local brandies better suited to cleaning rusty bicycle chains. Tuborg and Efes Pilsen bottled beers and lagers are easily available.

If there's a national liquor it has to be *raki* – sometimes known by the Turks as "lion's milk" because it's strong and goes white when you add water. Its aniseed taste is very like the Greek ouzo and the French pastis. Drink it neat if you've acquired the taste, or with water or soda.

Breakfast
Breakfast is normally crusty bread, olives, tomatoes, cucumber, perhaps a hard-boiled egg and cheese. The cheese might just be fresh sheep's cheese but it's usually one of those bland processed triangles in foil.

The larger tourist hotels are learning how to produce European breakfasts. One holidaymaker tells the tale of being asked by an eager-to-please hotel owner what the English have for breakfast. He suggested: "Boiled egg, scrambled eggs, fried eggs, bacon, sausage, toast . . ." Next morning, you've guessed it, the first person to ask for an English breakfast was served everything on the list, all on one plate.

In a hotel, you'll almost certainly get "European" tea for breakfast. Instant coffee – known as *Nes* whatever the brand – is now also served. The pensions and smaller hotels often charge extra for a cup of *Nes*.

Snacks

You see food sellers on the streets with their trolleys of snacks. Nuts are a favourite. So are peeled cucumbers served with salt and pepper and eaten like you would a banana. Roasted corn on the cob can be delicious. So can the sesame seed rolls called *simit* and bite-size syrupy pastries.

International food

If you're not happy with unknown and unusual food on holiday, remember that with tourists come chips and instant coffee. The longer a resort has been catering for foreign sun-worshippers, the more Italian pizzas, pina coladas and chips you'll find. The new resorts are catching up too. One tour rep told me how in one village that's isolated but on an excursion route she's just taught the restaurant owner to make chips. "That's what our holidaymakers want. Not everyone can cope with rich strange food every day for two weeks." Her next job is to teach him to serve the chips hot and at the same time as the fish.

The bread served at Turkish meals is freshly baked. If yours isn't, then the Turks are learning from the Spanish hoteliers faster than I'd thought.

Menu reader

Turkish menus with English translations are a hoot. Who could resist "Cold Brian", "Balls on fire", or "Wedding soap"? On a printed menu, usually only those dishes that have a price marked next to them are available. It's nearly always best to choose your meal from the display, not from the menu.

Here are some of the most famous and/or most common Turkish dishes that you may encounter:

- **düğün çorbasi** ("wedding soup"): a lamb broth flavoured with lemon and egg
- **işkembe çorbasi**: tripe soup – honestly! It's supposedly a good hangover cure
- **mercimek çorbasi**: lentil soup
- **pide**: unleavened bread, served with dips
- **humus**: chick-pea purée
- **tarama**: fish roe and oil purée
- **cacik**: chopped cucumber and garlic in yoghurt
- **patlican salatasi**: grilled aubergine puréed with lemon and yoghurt
- **patlican kizartmasi**: cold fried aubergine slices and yoghurt
- **imam bayildi** ("the priest fainted"): cold aubergines fried with onion, tomato, garlic and parsley
- **çoban salatasi**: mixed salad
- **borani**: spinach stewed with onion

- **bamya**: okra
- **biber**: peppers
- **domates**: tomatoes
- **enginar**: artichoke
- **fasulye**: beans
- **taze fasulye**: green beans
- **havuç**: carrots
- **ispanak**: spinach
- **mantar**: mushrooms
- **patates**: potatoes
- **patlican**: aubergine

- **arnavut ciğeri**: spiced fried liver and onion
- **peynirli börek**: light flaky pastry wrapped round cheese
- **kiymali börek**: the same but with minced meat

Dolma or **dolmasi** means stuffed (hence the word **dolmus** for those overcrowded taxis and minibuses). The stuffing is usually either rice, nuts and spices, or meat. The rice-stuffed vegetables are often served cold as a starter, the meat stuffed dishes, hot. **Etli** means stuffed with minced and spiced meat, so **biber dolmasi** is stuffed green peppers, but **etli biber dolmasi** is green peppers stuffed with meat.

- **etli domates dolmasi**: tomatoes stuffed with meat
- **etli kabak dolmasi**: marrow or courgette stuffed with meat
- **etli lahana dolmasi**: minced meat cooked in cabbage leaves
- **etli yaprak dolmasi**: stuffed vineleaves
- **etli patlican dolmasi**: aubergines stuffed with meat
- **şiş kebab**: lamb, green pepper and tomatoes grilled on a skewer
- **döner kebab**: grilled lamb or mutton roasted on an upright spit and carved into thin slices
- **ciğer kizartmasi**: fried liver
- **kuzu**: lamb
- **dana**: veal
- **etli patates**: meat with potatoes
- **etli sebze**: meat stew
- **hünhar beğendi** ("Sultan's delight"): aubergine purée with meat
- **köfte**: meatballs
- **içli köfte**: boiled and stuffed meatballs
- **izmir köftesi**: meatballs in tomato stew
- **kadin budu** ("ladies thighs"): fried meatballs made with minced lamb
- **oturtma**: aubergine casserole
- **tandir kebabi**: oven-cooked lamb with herbs
- **tavuk**: chicken

- **bulgur pilavi**: cracked wheat pilaf
- **iç pilav**: rice mixed with chopped liver, nuts, tomato and onion
- **sade pilav**: plain rice

Baliklar: fish. Not every fish you see on display has a straightforward translation. It's usually best to let your eye do the choosing
- **kalamar tava**: fried squid (like the Greek **calamares**)
- **midye**: mussels
- **midye tava**: fried mussels
- **balik köftesi**: fish balls
- **barbunya**: red mullet
- **hamsi**: anchovy, served grilled or fried
- **istako**: lobster
- **karides**: shrimp
- **kerevit**: prawn
- **kiliç**: swordfish – sometimes served smoked
- **levrek**: sea bass

Meyveleri: fruit
- **çilek**: strawberries
- **elma**: apple
- **incir**: figs
- **karpuz**: water-melon
- **kavun**: sweet melon
- **kiraz**: cherries
- **şeftali**: peaches
- **uzüm**: grapes

Talking your way through a meal
waiter	**garson**
waitress	**hanimefendi**
I'd like	**. . .istiyorum**
good	**iyi**
bad	**kötü**
fork	**çatal**
knife	**biçak**

spoon	kaşik
bill	hesap
How much is that?	Bu kaça?

bread	ekmek
butter	tereyaği
sugar	şeker
olive oil	zeytinyaği
salt	tuz
pepper (seasoning)	siyah biber
garlic	sarmisak

starter	meze
fish (one)	balik
meat	et

dessert, sweet	tatli
fruit (one)	meyva
salad	salata

cold	soğuk
hot	sicak
grilled	izgara
fried	tava
raw	çiğ
stuffed	dolma
well done	iyi pişmiş
medium rare	orta pişmiş
fresh	taze

drink	icki
soft drink	meşrubat
wine	şarap (sharrap)
red	kirmizi
white	beyaz
dry	sek
medium	domisek
coffee	kahve

(Turkish coffee is served in degrees of sweetness: **sade** is without sugar, **az** slightly sweetened, **orta** medium-sweet, **şekerli** sugary.)

sugar	**şeker**
tea	**çay** (chay)
gin	**cin**
vodka	**votka**
whisky	**viski**
beer	**bira**
fruit juice	**meyva suyu**
water	**su**
mineral water	**maden suyu**
fizzy water	**gazoz**
milk	**süt**

CHAPTER NINE: ISTANBUL

There's a reaction you commonly hear from someone visiting Istanbul for the first time: "I expected it to be exotic – but never *this* exotic." Istanbul is a powerful, alive, photogenic, confusing, chaotic, fascinating, romantic city. On the drive from the airport you might well wonder what you've come to visit. The leather tanneries on the approach roads can send out overwhelming stink-bomb fumes. The ramshackle dirty buildings must feature in any town planner's worst nightmare. The roads are criss-crossed with kamikaze drivers.

Then, after you've unpacked and freshened up, you take to the streets and over the choking exhaust fumes you catch that first whiff of Turkish tobacco and sizzling meats. You can just hear a *muezzin* calling from a mosque or some distinctive whining Turkish music, and you see the city views – familiar from a million dreamy paintings and photographs – of hills with mosques and minarets against a hazy sky.

Istanbul is about an hour's drive from the beach resort of Kilyos and three or four hours from Şile (although a motorway is planned between Istanbul and Şile for 1989-90, which should speed up the journey). It is possible to organise internal flights from Izmir, Dalaman and Antalya. A two-centre holiday with a stay in Istanbul followed by a week to recover on a beach offers the best of both worlds.

Sightseeing

It's not easy to get your bearings in Istanbul. On an

organised day's sightseeing, of course, you don't really need to. If you're staying for a few days you can fill each day with a different sightseeing tour which you can buy from hotels and tour operators. However, I recommend the more interesting experience of taking the city at your own pace, using a more detailed guide book, taxis and stout walking shoes. (If they're leather, have a shoeshine man polish the dust off at the end of the day.) You can buy good "Touristic City" maps of Istanbul in the city.

Everyone will have their own "musts", places they simply have to see. Here are my suggestions of the obvious ones.

After years of sightseeing, by the way, I'm a firm believer when time is short in seeing just three or four places in relaxed detail and taking time to watch the local life go by from a shady bench or cafe, rather than haring round everything and coming home with not too clear an idea of which palace was where, who built what and why.

The three most famous "musts" – *Topkapi Palace*, the *Sultan Ahmet Mosque* (which most people call the Blue Mosque) and *St Sophia* – are close together in the Sultan Ahmet area on the Old Istanbul side of the Golden Horn. The fourth "must", the *Grand Bazaar*, is a walk away (or a cab ride if your feet have given up). The Dolmabahçe Palace is on the "New Side" of Istanbul.

Topkapi Palace

The Topkapi Palace was first built in the fifteenth century by Mehmet the Conqueror, and added to by each sultan after him. It ended up as a sort of royal village with its own schools, gardens, fountains, mosques, bath houses and four main courtyards. The household was moved to the new and more Westernised Dolmabahçe Palace in 1853, when Sultan Abdül Mecit wanted to show the world how "European" he could be.

The *Harem*, I think, is the highlight of a visit to the palace. However, if you're not in an organised sightseeing party you need to get a separate entrance ticket to join a guided tour round the harem and these can sell out early in the day. Independent visitors to the palace should head straight for the Harem ticket booth (the earlier in the morning, the better) which is in the Court of the Divan. Ask to join an English-speaking tour. Your ticket will have the time of your Harem tour stamped on it.

The rooms in the Harem are exquisitely decorated with tiles and stained glass. The Harem is designed to catch the precious cooling summer breezes and there's a surprising cosiness about the place. One can only wonder in astonishment at the private lives of the sultans, their wives (each sultan was allowed up to four), their mother (who in effect ruled the roost and often the empire), the concubines and the eunuchs. The wives vied with each other to produce a male heir who would inherit the throne – and thus make them Queen Mother. The concubines vied with each other to catch the eye of the sultan and then to share his pillow. Others worked hard to avoid his eye because at age 25, if they were still untouched by his lordship, they could leave if they wanted.

Anyway, this is where they all lived until 1853, when the Harem was moved to the Dolmabahçe Palace. It was disbanded in 1909, when Abdül Hamid was deposed. Even then, when Edward VII was on the British throne, there were 213 people living in the Harem. The last surviving female was reputed to be still alive, heavily veiled and living in Istanbul, in 1970.

Elsewhere in the palace you can visit the *kitchens*, which once fed five thousand people a day. The huge cauldrons and cooking pots give you an idea of the amount of food they got through. The recipes of some of the dishes you'll be eating on holiday were first concocted and perfected in these kitchens. There's a priceless collection of porcelain on display, including some intriguing plates reputed to change colour when touched by poison. Just the gift for the sultan who has everything.

The display in the *Treasury* is world-famous. Here you can stare at all the diamonds, emeralds and jade that the Ottomans came to hoard. The jewel-encrusted dagger –

made famous in the old film *Topkapi* – the 86-carat Spoonmaker's Diamond and many of the other jewels are so large it's hard to believe that they're genuine. They look for all the world like costume jewellery for a school play. Aladdin perhaps? The Spoonmaker's Diamond is so called because it was found by a beggar who handed it over for three wooden spoons.

If you're not in a group, try to visit the Treasury first thing in the morning before you have to jostle for a peep at the treasure with tour groups of all nationalities.

Other displays in the Palace include costumes, glassware and silverware, weapons and holy relics of the prophet Mohammed. There's a restaurant which serves drinks and snacks but which gets busy with tour groups at lunchtimes. It offers a panoramic view of the Bosphorus, the entrance to the Golden Horn waterway and the Sea of Marmara.

Topkapi Palace is closed on Tuesdays. Most other museums in Turkey close on Mondays.

Sultan Ahmet Mosque – The Blue Mosque

The Blue Mosque is the only one in the world with six minarets. It was built between 1609 and 1616 and the story goes that the architect misheard the Sultan's order for the minarets to be built of gold – the word for "gold" being similar to the word for "six". Or did he only pretend to mishear because he and his advisors didn't want to empty the treasury of gold? Inside the dome, the pillars and the walls are covered with intricate tiles in 99 shades of blue – 99 being a holy number in Islam. There are over 21,000 ceramic tiles. As in all mosques, you'll need to leave your shoes outside (you get used to the whiff of tourists' feet). The floor is covered with rugs given as presents to the mosque. If you're wearing shorts you'll be lent a cloth to cover your legs.

St Sophia

Opposite the Blue Mosque is the powerful St Sophia, built as a Christian church in the sixth century by the Emperor

Justinian on the spot where Constantine the Great was reputed to have built a basilica. Before that, it was supposed to have been the site of a pagan temple. Justinian commandeered the finest materials available for this building, which is an astonishing tribute to the Golden Age of the Byzantine Empire. Four acres of the walls and ceilings were covered with decorative mosaics – each with up to six thousand pieces per square foot.

In the early thirteenth century the Crusaders plundered the church and robbed it of its gold and silver treasures. The minarets were added when the Ottoman Turks converted the church to a mosque nearly one thousand years after it was built, in 1453. By good fortune, the plaster they used to cover the Christian mosaics turned out to be just the substance to preserve them. St Sophia is now officially a museum and not a working mosque. In the upstairs gallery you can see charming mosaics of the Holy Family. St Sophia gives you an awesome sense of the history of Istanbul and just how the different cultures have used this city as the centre of world power.

If you're not on a whirlwind tour there's much more exploring you can do in the Sultan Ahmet area. For a rest, there are pretty gardens, flowerbeds of hollyhocks and marigolds. There's a relaxed pavement cafe that offers shade and drinks and snacks at reasonable prices even though it's in the thick of the tourist area.

Alongside the Topkapi Palace and by the side of St Sophia, along an alley called *Soğukçeşme Sokağı*, there's a row of newly renovated wooden Ottoman houses, painted in pastel colours. Some are now hotels and are open for drinks and snacks to non-residents. The Sarnic at the bottom of the street is a basement restaurant in a high-domed Roman water storage cistern. (Istanbul has always had to bring in its water and rely on springs because there is no river in the city.) The restaurant is impressive to look at although the food and the live music tries to be "international" – with prices to match.

The street in front of the Blue Mosque is in fact part of

There are minarets like exclamation marks all over Istanbul - but the Blue Mosque is the only building with six of them.

the old *Hippodrome* – a chariot racing stadium first built in 203 and enlarged by Constantine. This was where they held the opening ceremony for the founding of New Rome. There's little left today of the stadium, which could seat 100,000, but you can still see the top of the *Obelisk of Theodosius*, carved in Egypt some time around 1500 BC, the *Bronze Serpentine Column* which Constantine brought from Delphi and which is the oldest Greek monument in the city and an *Obelisk of Bricks*.

The *Archaeological Museum* is by the Topkapi Palace in a courtyard, with the Tile Museum displayed in the oldest non-religious building in Istanbul – the *Çinili Köşkü* built by Mehmet the Conqueror in 1472 – and next to the *Museum of the Ancient Order*. The museums are open from nine to five every day, but closed on Monday except in high summer.

On the other side of the Hippodrome from the Blue Mosque, the *İbrahim Pasa Museum*, the Turkish and Islamic Arts Museum, includes Turkish and Persian miniatures, carpets and tiles from the eighth century onwards. It is housed in the stone palace of Süleyman's son-in-law.

If you're interested in waterworks, the *Yerebatan Sarayi* is a vast underground man-made water storage cistern built in the sixth century by the Emperor Justinian. There are 336 Corinthian columns supporting the brick vaulting.

Along the side of the gardens is a reconstructed Turkish Bath (*hamam*) commissioned by Süleyman the Magnificent for his wife Roxana.

However many – or few – of the sights you visit in this area, I do recommend you come back at night for a stroll round and maybe a drink in one of the cafes. Obviously the buildings are closed, but St Sophia and the Blue Mosque are lit up and look stunning.

The Bazaar
A must – even if you loathe shopping. This covered shopping town of pedestrian streets and alleyways was founded in 1461 by Mehmet the Conqueror, although many

of the streets you'll be walking along and their vaulted roofs have been rebuilt after earthquakes and more recently after a major fire in 1954. The glass shop-fronts and the strip lighting are obviously new but the design of the bazaar hasn't changed over the centuries. The feel of the place can't have changed much either.

Many a lad will offer to be your guide and then will take you to his favoured shops (and cream off a commission from the shopkeeper on whatever you buy). You don't need him. The shops are a mix of serious jewellery, carpet and antique shops and hustling shops of bags, slippers and fake designer shirts, brasswear and ceramics. You need to bargain (see chapter seven on shopping).

Resign yourself to getting lost. Most traders speak English (and German and French and American) and someone can usually point the way to the main exit. There are cafes for drinks and snacks in the bazaar and on the right just before you enter the building from the main entrance there's a tiny, busy shop that sells tumblers of freshly-squeezed orange juice.

For more peaceful, leisurely browsing when you've escaped from the bazaar, look for the *Book Market* (Sahaflar Çarşisi). It's set in a shady courtyard and offers a mixture, from exotic copies of the Koran to Turkish cookery books and second-hand Agatha Christies. You can also buy postcards here and maybe write them in the tea gardens through the courtyard behind the Beyazit Mosque.

Spice Market

The Spice Market – sometimes called the Egyptian Bazaar – is much smaller than the Grand Bazaar. It's near the large Yeni Cami – New Mosque – built in 1663 – in a lively area that's a sort of unofficial open air market near the waterfront along the Golden Horn in the Eminönü district. Inside the covered Spice Market which was built in 1571 you can see and smell great sacks of colourful herbs and spices, nuts and dried fruits. There are tiny shops crammed with many different sorts of Turkish Delights and cakes.

For lunch you could try the Pandeli restaurant in the market (telephone 522 55 34). You'll find its entrance up the stairs which are tucked away to the left of the main entrance as you enter through the arch. The waiters are used to foreign tour groups so they can be pretty brisk and the menu I was given was in German, Italian and Turkish, but the original tiled decor of the restaurant is charming. The Pandeli has been serving food in this room since the early eighteenth century.

Dolmabahçe Palace

The Dolmabahçe Palace is included in many sightseeing tours. It stands with its own marble quayside beside the Bosphorus across the Golden Horn from the Sultan Ahmet area. The palace is not too far from Taksim Square where the large modern hotels are.

You are not allowed to wander around the palace on your own. You have to wait in the main reception hall for a guided tour. The palace was built in the mid-nineteenth century by Sultan Abdül Mecit to replace Topkapi and to show the world that the Turkish nation was "civilised". It was therefore built of white marble to outdo other European grand palaces and it's full of musty and dusty Victorian paraphernalia and faded portraits. There are 36 chandeliers and a staircase with crystal banisters. And of course there's the Harem. When Turkey became a republic, Atatürk took a small apartment here. The simple bedroom where he died in 1938 is part of the tour and the clock has been stopped at 9.05 to mark the time of his death. The palace has pleasant gardens and a garden cafe for drinks.

Sailing the Bosphorus

Some of the most impressive views of Istanbul are from the water. Sightseeing excursions that include a boat trip along the Bosphorus towards the Black Sea are deservedly popular. Usually the boats head for a large village like Beylerbeyi on the Asian side of the straits. As you approach it, Europe is on your left, Asia on your right, and on the

There are still a few traditional wooden houses along the banks of the Bosphorus. Take a ferry trip between Europe and Asia.

banks you can see the few remaining traditional wooden houses that are now being renovated and sold for millions – of pounds not lire! When the boat stops at Beylerbeyi you can visit the new tourist shops or just stroll along the front and stop for a drink or a snack of grilled corn on the cob. You'll want your camera for the views of Istanbul when you sail back along the Golden Horn.

You can take a local ferry for a trip along the Bosphorus and back. The ferries leave from the docks by the Galata Bridge but, except for winter, they are crowded and you need to board early to get a seat.

Tarabya

Because taxis, ferries and buses cost so little, a trip out for an evening meal along the Bosphorus is feasible and fun. It takes about half an hour by taxi from central Istanbul to the seaside harbour of Tarabya. (The cost in summer 1988 was around 6500 TL one way.) The front is lined with restaurants and in summer the tables spread out onto the pavement. There's a bustling Riviera feel to the place, with horse-drawn open carriages, boats bobbing on the water, veiled women on holiday from the Arab states, a stream of men selling nuts and nibbles, and wide-eyed little children trying to persuade the male diners to buy their companions a bunch of roses.

Most restaurants have a display of the day's fishing catch and you can choose what you wish to eat. Stroll along the front comparing restaurants and prices and ignoring the waiters hustling for business. Some places like the Palet have live music. By ten or eleven at night, when the restaurants are full, exotic Turkish dancing starts to break out among the diners on the little dance floor. There are usually plenty of taxis around when you finally feel you have to head back to the smoke.

Istanbul hotels

The package holiday companies offer a good selection of

prices. At the top end come the "international" luxury hotels, the Etap Marmara and the Sheraton in the Taksim Square area. For a price they offer an air-conditioned escape (with swimming pools and hot baths) from the grimy, noisy, confusing city. The Etap Marmara has a posh bar, nightclub and restaurant at the top of the hotel, all open to non-residents. You might like to spruce up and sip a cocktail at the rooftop bar and watch the sun go down over the panoramic view of the city.

Romantics with cash who don't demand air conditioning choose the Pera Palace in the more run-down Tepebasi area overlooking the Golden Horn. This recently renovated treasure was built in 1892 for passengers from the Orient Express. Agatha Christie stayed here and polished off her novel *Murder on the Orient Express*. There's a suite of rooms that Atatürk used which has been kept as a museum. If you're visiting for drinks in the elegant bar or on the terrace, have a good look round and make sure you peer into the lift!

There are many small and serviceable hotels used by the tour operators in the city. The ones nearest to the major sights are obviously the most convenient.

Getting around

Taxis are much cheaper than in British cities. Your hotel can advise on the average cost of a particular journey. Make sure the driver switches on his meter. Some drivers are kind and friendly. Others see tourists as easy game. Outside the bazaar, for example, two drivers demanded 7000 TL for a journey I knew cost only around 1200. They wouldn't budge without me first agreeing. So I didn't and found a different driver. Not many taxi drivers speak English. It helps to know the district you want.

Istanbul traffic jams have to be seen to be believed. Always allow plenty of time to get anywhere – especially during the rush hour. Crossing a main road is a challenge. Your best bet is to mingle with a group of locals and cross when they do. A coach driver in Istanbul explained to me how some drivers have indeed noticed those red and green lights by the crossroads. They think they make quite pretty decorations.

For bus rides, you need to buy tickets from the kiosks at the bus stations or main transfer points. The main stations are at Sirkeci Station, Eminönü on the old city side of the Galata Bridge, and Taksim Square. The *dolmus* minibuses also offer a cramped but very cheap way of getting around the city. See also chapter six on Getting around.

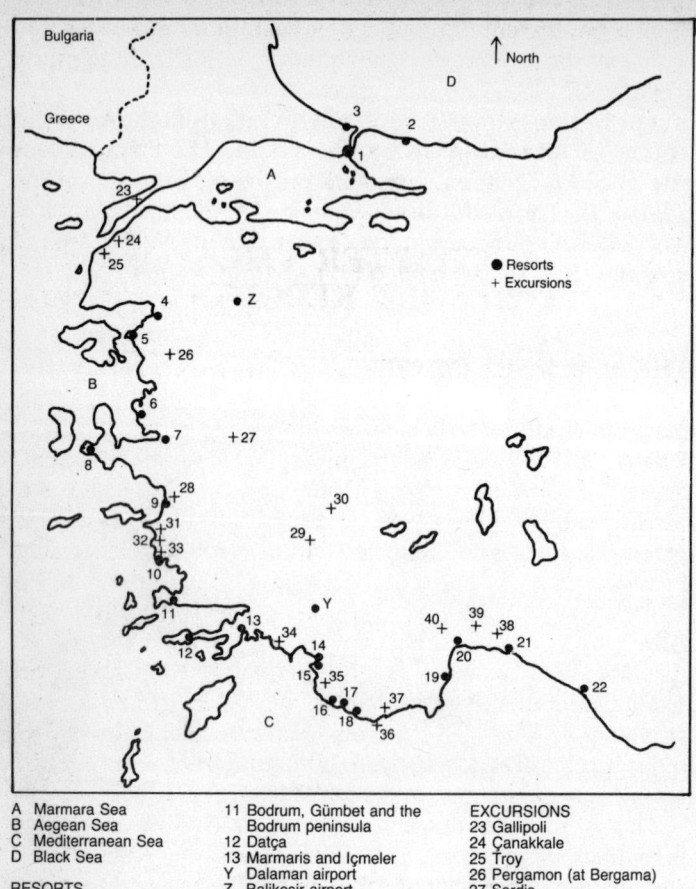

A Marmara Sea
B Aegean Sea
C Mediterranean Sea
D Black Sea

RESORTS
1 Istanbul
2 Şile
3 Kilyos
4 Ören
5 Ayvalik
6 Foça
7 Izmir and Izmir airport
8 Çeşme
9 Kuşadasi
10 Altinkum
11 Bodrum, Gümbet and the Bodrum peninsula
12 Datça
13 Marmaris and Içmeler
Y Dalaman airport
Z Balikesir airport
14 Fethiye
15 Ölü Deniz
16 Patara
17 Kalkan
18 Kaş
19 Kemer
20 Antalya and Antalya airport
21 Side
22 Alanya

EXCURSIONS
23 Gallipoli
24 Çanakkale
25 Troy
26 Pergamon (at Bergama)
27 Sardis
28 Ephesus
29 Aphrodisias
30 Pamukkale
31 Priene
32 Miletus
33 Didyma
34 Dalyan and Caunos
35 Xanthos and Letoon
36 Kekova
37 Demre
38 Aspendos
39 Perge
40 Termessos

Western Turkey: the major holiday resorts and the sights to see.

CHAPTER TEN: RESORT REPORTS

THE BLACK SEA COAST

You can find the following resorts in one or more of the British package holiday brochures. There is more rainfall around the Black Sea than on the Aegean and Mediterranean coasts. As a result, the countryside is greener and lusher. The resorts in this area can occasionally be cloudy.

Şile

Şile is about two hours from Istanbul (depending on Istanbul's dreadful traffic) and it will be less when a new, straighter road is finished. It's a small ramshackle town. The older, pretty basic hotels were built about ten years ago for townies from Istanbul who spent the weekend here.

There are steps down to a large beach with sand that is supposed to have a healing effect on sciatica and rheumatism. There are snack bars on the beach. There are quiet coves and beaches along the coast outside Şile, but you'll need a taxi to reach them – there's nowhere yet to hire cars or mopeds.

In the small town centre there are smaller restaurants with even smaller terraces built on stilts and overlooking the harbour. The local men spend the evenings in the main open-air cafe watching bootleg videos. Shopping is pretty limited: for anything other than the basics you need to travel into Istanbul. Şile is the manufacturing centre for *Şilebezi*, a cotton gauze fabric which you can buy made up into tops and dresses.

British holidaymakers started coming here on packages in 1988. Entries in the visitor's book in one of the hotels keep mentioning the "friendly, obliging" locals. Not a place for luxury stays or dressing up at night.

Kilyos

Kilyos is an hour or so from Istanbul, which makes it very popular with Turks from the city at weekends and on public holidays. The Hotel Turban has its own beach but if you're not staying there it costs 2000 TL (1988 price) to get onto the main sandy beach. There are markers in the sea showing where there can be dangerous undercurrents – dangerous enough for people to drown. One holiday rep whispered to me that 15 people (mostly locals in winter) drowned here in 1987.

Until 1988, package holiday tourists to Kilyos came from Germany. There's no swish nightlife and the shops stock just the basics. At weekends and some evenings, open-air restaurants set up in the fields along the road outside Kilyos. Turkish families come for the day. Sometimes the restauranteurs organise pony rides for children and there's a sort of gymkhana atmosphere. You can buy roast meats from the spit, salads and drinks.

It's possible to buy organised day trips to Istanbul from Kilyos, or you can take a *dolmus* along the coast and then catch a ferry into the city.

THE AEGEAN COAST (FROM NORTH TO SOUTH)

Oren

Oren is very much a holiday town for the Turkish – so far. It's not a high-rise resort, but then, few in Turkey are. There's a lot of greenery about the town which makes it quite attractive. The beach is long, sandy and clean, with windsurfing and sailing.

A plaza on the seafront is the main meeting place. Because British tourism is so new here (Sunmed feature it for the first time in the 1989 brochure) the restaurants serve mainly Turkish food. No hamburgers and pizzas – yet. No wild or very late nightlife and hardly any British pop music.

Transfer time from Balikesir airport is an hour and a half (Balikesir opened for British charter flights for the first time in 1989.)

Ayvalik
Ayvalik is a thriving, busy old commercial town that could survive very well if there were suddenly no tourists. It has olive oil and soap-making industries, a fishing centre and a terminus for boats over to Mytilini on the Greek island of Lesbos.

Ayvalik was inhabited by Ottoman Greeks until the end of World War One, when they were exchanged with Turks from Crete. Today you can see how one mosque was a Greek Orthodox church until they built on some minarets. You can travel by boat or across a causeway to the small island of Ali Bey, where there are some fish restaurants.

Seytan Sofrasi – "the devil's dinner table" – is not far. It offers a glorious view over the bay and islands. The beach is Sarimsakli (clean sand and shingle), 2½ miles long and about two miles out of town.

Nightlife in Ayvalik is traditional Turkish – eating, talking and some Turkish music. There are plenty of shops packed into the town. Ayvalik is near Bergama, the ancient city of Pergamum. See the chapter on excursions.

Transfer time from Balikesir airport is two hours, or you can fly to Izmir, which is further away.

Foça
Foça is a pleasant small port used by French tourists. There's a Club Med there, but even so, it's one of the more peaceful resorts. Evenings are pretty quiet in Foça. There's no beach to speak of, just a small shingle patch at one end of the bay. There is a sandy beach about two miles along the

road, with a *dolmus* service to this beach and to other bays along the coast.

In ancient times, Foça was the Ionian city of Phocaia. Around the sixth century, Phocaians colonised parts of the Mediterranean coast, including the ports now known as Marseilles and Nice.

Transfer time from Izmir is one and a half to two hours.

Çeşme

Çeşme lies 50 miles west of Izmir, on a peninsula opposite the Greek island of Chios, which is a six-mile boat trip away. It's a tourist town, although as yet only one of the large British tour operators sells holidays there.

The resort sprawls below bare limestone rocks, with hotels and rooms along the beach roads and village centres at the different beaches. Çeşme itself hasn't much beach, but those nearby have soft sand and gentle slopes with safe swimming. Ilica is a popular wide beach about a mile from Çeşme.

Çeşme town has restaurants along the waterfront by the harbour, which is being developed into a holiday marina. There's a fortress overlooking the harbour that was built by the Genoese in the fourteenth century. It was done up in the sixteenth century by the son of Mehmet the Conqueror, Beyazit, who used it to defend the coast against pirates and the Knights of St John from Rhodes. There's now a small museum at the castle. An ancient caravanserai has been converted into a hotel – the Çeşme Kervansaray.

The name Çeşme means a spring or fountain and the town was originally a spa where visitors came to take the hot thermal waters which bubble into the sea at certain points along the coast here. In summer there's an annual Turkish song contest and a folklore sea festival. You can take boat trips for the day from Çeşme to other beaches and coves, and there are day excursions to Ephesus – but it's a long trip. There are smaller and nearer historical sites on the peninsula at Erythrai and Teos. Both are charming and uncommercialised.

The transfer from Izmir airport takes around two hours.

Kuşadasi

Kuşadasi developed as a holiday resort because it's so close to the major archaeological site of Ephesus. Anyone even remotely interested in great sights of the world wants to see Ephesus (see chapter eleven). Kuşadasi port grew to accommodate the cruise ships that drop off their passengers for a day's sightseeing. Kuşadasi town grew when mass tourism first came to the country, and it's still growing.

The worst – or for many people, the best – thing about Kuşadasi is that it's past the stage of being a Turkish port that takes summer tourists. It's now a holiday resort that happens to be in Turkey. This means that you don't have to eat Turkish food or listen to Turkish music or even talk much to Turks. Here you can get by, if you want, with sun and beach, Bros and Madonna, chips and pizza. It's almost as if the place is being stripped of its Turkishness – and then special Turkish trimmings like carpet shops, horse-drawn carriages and belly dancing evenings are being installed to amuse the visitors. However, Kuşadasi is still years away from being a Benidorm.

There's a pleasant prom and an excellent marina choc-a-bloc with international yachts. There are masses of shops in the Grand Bazaar. With so many day trippers as well as stay-put holidaymakers there would be, wouldn't there? The salesmen are well used to cruise passengers who have no time to shop around and prices are hiked up accordingly. There's a restored Ottoman Caravanserai which is now a hotel. You can visit for drinks.

The name Kuşadasi, as every brochure tells you, means Island of Birds (or Pigeons). The island has a small fourteenth-century fortress and is linked to the town with a causeway. The discos and many bars on the island frightened off most birds years ago.

Kadinlar, about two miles south of Kuşadasi, is a slightly more traditional resort, in an area that's steep and hilly. The name means "ladies' beach" but that was years ago. Today's

There's "traditional" Turkish entertainment at nights in every large resort.

beach, sandy and gently sloping, gets very crowded in summer. There are watersports, music from the beach bars and Turks trying to sell you things. A firm but pleasant No should move them on. Better still, avoid eye contact and ignore them.

Güzelçamli is about 16 miles south of Kuşadasi and near the National Millipark which has pretty coves and beaches. The park gets very crowded with Turkish holidaymakers in August, at weekends and on public holidays.

Kuşadasi is opposite the Greek island of Samos where Pythagoras was born. In summer you can take a boat trip over for the day. Ephesus is 20 minutes from Kuşadasi. Pamukkale is a long day's excursion inland.

Transfer time from Izmir should be two hours.

Altinkum

It was the beach and the atmosphere at Altinkum that first convinced Sunmed boss Vic Fatah he was right to sell beach holidays to Turkey.

Altinkum means "golden" and the beach is long, clean and sandy. The sea is safe and shallow for a good way out, and suitable for windsurfing. Behind the beach there's a busy but relaxed resort growing up, with plenty of bars and restaurants catering for all tastes. Nightlife is lively, if casual and unsophisticated. Prices are lower than in Kuşadasi. Altinkum is rightly popular at weekends and high summer with holidaying Turks.

About three miles away is Didyma, once the site of a glorious temple of Apollo and a sacred sanctuary for priests. At one time it was a serious rival to the famous shrine and oracle at Delphi. Croesus – the rich one – came here for consultations, as did the Egyptian Pharoah Necho. The temple you gawp at today replaced the original one which was destroyed by Persians. This temple, built in the fourth century AD, has been well excavated and partly restored. From the site there are wonderful views of the coast.

Transfer time to Altinkum from Izmir is around two and a half hours.

Bodrum

Bodrum is now a major holiday resort – very pretty and very popular. It's famous for its handsome medieval castle which juts out on the waterfront between two bays. In the holiday world it's probably now equally famous for its cosmopolitan and sophisticated atmosphere. There's no real beach in Bodrum. For that, you have to travel two miles or so to Gümbet, or to any other of the places now springing up as resorts around the Bodrum peninsula.

In the town there are palm trees along the front and a harbour where the wooden *gulets* (see chapter twelve) squeeze in alongside the gin palaces ("raki palaces" doesn't have the same ring) of the rich international yacht set. The back streets are loaded with restaurants, bars and stalls selling souvenirs and fake designer sportswear. Shopping in Bodrum is very good and comprehensive – from sponges and barbecue skewers to top-quality designer leathers.

Bodum has a pacy nightlife. The Halicarnassus laser disco on the front is supposed to be one of the best in Europe, and there are upbeat bars where you can show off your designer T-shirts. Some of the fish restaurants on the front near the castle have especially good reputations. Prices are higher than in the backstreet places.

Many *gulet* cruises start from Bodrum. You can also buy day-long boat trips, including an excursion to the Greek island of Kos. Bodrum's well-preserved Crusader castle is one of the finest in the world. It has five towers built by knights from five countries: England, France, Spain, Germany and Itay. The English tower now contains a British "pub" with waitresses in St John cloaks! The place is dotted with statues and artefacts from the area and there's a notable underwater archaeology collection of antiquities found in ships on the seabed. In September Bodrum hosts an annual cultural festival, with shows in the castle's open-air theatre. There are markets every Thursday and Friday.

In ancient times Bodrum, then known as Halicarnassus, was an important city. It was founded by Dorian Greeks around 1200 BC. The Persians took it over in 540 BC and a Persian leader called Mausolus ordered his burial chamber, a great stepped pyramid of marble, to be built in the city. This mighty tomb – known as the Mausoleum – was one of the seven wonders of the ancient world (for the other six see the notes about Ephesus), and ever since the word has been used for any large burial chamber. Today you can see the excavated site and a plaster model of the original Mausoleum.

The Greek writer Herodotus, the one they call the "father of history" because he was the first to write down a factual account of past events, was born in Bodrum in 485 BC. The Romans got their hands on the town in 129 BC. Then it became part of the Byzantine Empire in AD 395, and in 1402 was conquered by the Knights Hospitallers of St John, who built the Castle of St Peter using some of the stones from the Mausoleum.

Transfer time to Bodrum from Dalaman airport is around three hours, from Izmir three and a half.

Gümbet

There have been some hotels established for a few years at Gümbet, two miles west of Bodrum, but more recently the place has been doing a great impersonation of a Turkish building site. It's an obvious spot for the holiday industry to grow because, unlike Bodrum, it has a beach (dark, sandy and narrow) with a choice of watersports available. It's a hilly resort, with bars and cafes along the beach. Don't expect to find neat pavements and smooth roads. Gümbet is scrappy now. It could be fine when it's finished.

The Bodrum peninsula

As Bodrum isn't allowed to expand upwards – new buildings are restricted to two storeys – it's expanding sideways, right round the Bodrum peninsula in fact. Since 1988 a handful of small seaside villages new to tourism have appeared in the brochures. Each one is going to get bigger until one day, no doubt, they'll all join up. Meanwhile each place is OK if you

Fast food, Turkish style.

want somewhere quiet with a few places to eat (most will be newly-opened cafes), a sandy beach, not much to do and a *dolmus* ride into Bodrum when you want shops, sights and nightlife.

Before you book, decide just how near you want to be to the bright lights of Bodrum. Some places are not "just up the road". The newly popular *Turgutries*, for example, is 11 miles away. Turgutries is peaceful but the seabed drops deeply quite near to the shore so it's not a good beach for young children.

Other newly popular resorts include *Gümüşlük* which is tiny and still unspoilt. The sand is grey and coarse and the water is so shallow you can wade out to nearby Rabbit Island. Gümüşlük is an official archeaological site so there shouldn't be any new building work starting. *Güvercinlik* is also small and pretty but there are no restrictions against putting up new buildings! There's no beach here, just concrete jetties. The very busy coast road runs through the place.

The transfer time from the airport to some of the resorts on the Bodrum penisula can take up to five hours.

Datça

Datça is stuck out on a narrow, very attractive peninsula 50 miles west of Marmaris. The winding hilly road that leads to Datça has some lovely views. Along the peninsula there are beaches and campsites. Datça itself is small but expanding, with new small hotels, rooms and shops being built. It's a casual, inexpensive resort. What beach there is, however, is coarse sand and shingle. You can swim off the bays in clear shallow waters. There's a pretty yacht harbour and a ferry service over to Bodrum. I've been told that the waters around here are popular with dolphins.

On the tip of the peninsula, 22 miles west of Datça, are the ruins at Knidos. You can get there by road and track or, more fun, by boat. Knidos used to be a centre of learning and art and had a famous medical school. Sir Charles Newton from Britain organised the first excavations in the nineteenth century so, needless to say, most of the statues and sculptures from the site are in London at the British Museum. The tip of the peninsula is opposite the Greek island of Kos.

Transfer time to Datça from Dalaman airport is three and a half hours.

MEDITERRANEAN COAST
(FROM NORTH TO SOUTH)

Marmaris

There's obviously no marked border between the Aegean Sea and the Mediterranean but it's generally agreed that they merge around Marmaris. There's a Riviera feel to Marmaris. It has a European-style palm-lined promenade and one of the largest marinas in Turkey. The Turkish glitterati have been coming here for some time now and more recently the European glitzy set have taken to parking their million-dollar yachts in Marmaris marina.

As a result, Marmaris has the ideal set-up for classical Mediterranean nights: a stroll at dusk along the front, wistfully admiring the boats, followed by cocktails in a first-floor bar overlooking the marina. Another stroll comparing menus, accompanied by the patter of the waiters eager to pull you into their restaurant. A meal, and then drinks or a dance at a loud music bar. The restaurants on the waterfront are more expensive than those in the back streets. There is a town beach (sand and shingle). It's nothing special and it gets very crowded. You can pay a few lire to enter Atatürk Park along the front which has a beach and shallow water.

From Marmaris you can pick up a *gulet* cruise. There are boat trips for the day on offer, including trips to other beaches, over to Fethiye or out to Cleopatra Island. The story goes that Mark Antony had the fine sand on Cleopatra Island specially brought over from the Black Sea coast – at least, that's what they tell you. The boat trip to Rhodes takes about three hours.

Marmaris is a noisy town. The music bars are open until the last bopper drops. At dawn the *muezzin* whines his call to prayer. In summer there's an annual Festival of Music and Art.

In ancient times, Marmaris was known as Physkos. It was a port with a good trade to Egypt via Rhodes. There's little sightseeing in the town itself. (For important sites around the area see chapter eleven on excursions.) There are the ruins of a fifteenth-century fortress on the hill and an Ottoman caravanserai, once a watering hole for travelling silk merchants and now a souvenir shopping centre.

Transfer time to Marmaris from Dalaman airport is around an hour and a half. Fethiye and Bodrum are each about three hours away by bus.

Içmeler

As a holiday town Marmaris has spread out along the cost road as far as the next bay, Içmeler, which the holiday brochures now acknowledge as a resort in its own right. There are hotels all along the coast road from Marmaris to Içmeler: small family-run ones and larger holiday village complexes. From some of them along this stretch you have to cross the busy main road to get to the beach.

Until very recently you could have described Içmeler itself as a tiny village with a small fishing harbour. Not any more. It's now a full holiday resort that's getting bigger week by week. New hotels and accommodation blocks are being pushed up apparently at random on the wide area between the beach (dark sand with shingle, sunbeds and umbrellas for hire, watersports, drinks and snacks) and the pine-covered hills behind the bay. The new accommodation is of a good standard for Turkey, Many hotels have their own pools and disco nightlife. There's limited shopping.

If there's a master plan to the design of the new Içmeler resort, I can't work out what it is. Who knows? Someone somewhere may be working on a plan for pavements and such. Meanwhile, be prepared for dusty walks and building works. An unfinished symphony of concrete?

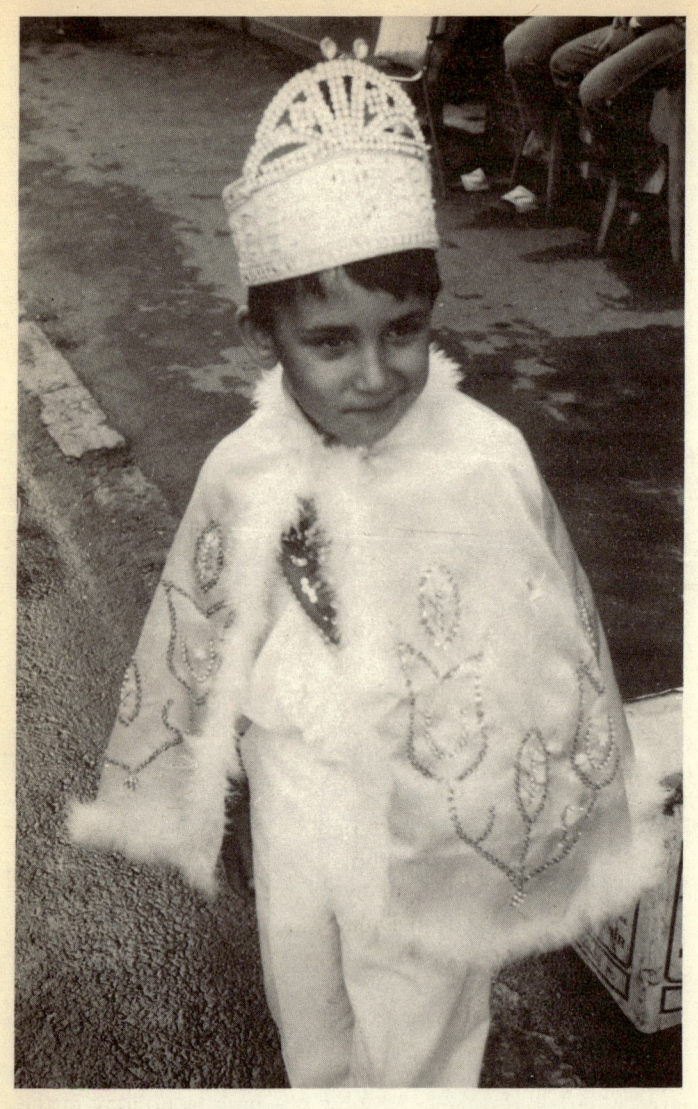

Every Turkish Moslem boy becomes a King for a week as part of his growing up.

It takes fifteen to twenty minutes by taxi from Içmeler to Marmaris centre.

Ölü Deniz

Five years ago Ölü was an empty beach by a lagoon, with one hotel, some camp sites and a few wooden sheds or "chalets" in brochure speak. Now this beautiful bay features in holiday advertisements in magazines and there are more new rooms for holidaymakers than there are beehives in the pine woods. The white beach is a long sweep of pale shingle. The now famous lagoon has been designated an Area of Outstanding Natural Beauty and the few lire you pay to enter through its wire fence go towards its upkeep.

Along the beach there are casual *locantas* where you can eat and drink. Many of the rooms on the beach are in tiny wooden sheds put up on what used to be camp sites for Scandinavian and German backpackers. With the exception of the beachside Hotel Ölü Deniz, the new accommodation is along the road away from the beach, up the hill. The older Hotel Meri on the lagoon was built to cater for German tourists and its restaurant reflects their tastes. They've rigged up a loudspeaker system for relaying music to sunbathers on their bit of the beach. Back in 1986 the charming, smiling receptionist was proudly showing everyone the visitor's book. As he didn't read English he was unaware of the rather coarse criticisms entered by disgruntled guests. I'm told that the hotel has since been refurbished and I bet the book is no longer on display.

Ölü is about half an hour by taxi or *dolmus* from Fethiye and ninety minutes from Dalaman airport.

Fethiye

Fethiye is a busy, very Turkish port built round a harbour. Until now the locals have, on the whole, been wide-eyed and unsoured by the tourists. How they will cope with the large numbers of foreigners now planning to holiday in the town in summer remains to be seen. There's no beach in Fethiye. Çaliş beach (pebbles, shingle and sand) is about ten minutes by taxi. There's windsurfing and waterskiing available. Hotels and holiday rooms are strung all along the Çaliş beach road, so Çaliş is not really a resort with its own centre.

In Fethiye there's good shopping and eating in the narrow back streets. At night there's a bustling atmosphere around the restaurants. There are some Lycian tombs to look at up on the hill at the back of the town. A word of warning. Unless the masseurs have succumbed to the needs of frail European tourists and changed their ways, a Turkish massage at the ancient baths in Fethiye is, well, very Turkish. Europeans of both sexes use the same room. When it's your turn for a rub-down you're spread onto the centre stone, lathered up, and pummelled and cleaned in every nook and cranny. A bruising experience and not one for the prudish. You also lose the top layer of your suntan.

A shave and/or a shampoo at the barber's is more relaxing. If Fethi Sener is still there on the corner opposite the Yapi Kredi bank near the Otel Kaya, get one of the lads to wash your hair (ladies) or give you a shave (men). Then ask for his massage. (You might have to mime this request.) A good working over from the top of your head, down your arms and across the shoulders is the best hangover cure in the country. The haircuts aren't bad either.

Transfer time to Fethiye from Dalaman airport is around ninety minutes.

The coast from Fethiye to Kaş is sometimes called the **Lycian Peninsula**. It's an exceptionally beautiful coastline, littered with ancient sites and remains. Holidaymakers in firm shoes have been known to scramble off the beaten track, brush away the dust to sit down and discover bits of a mosaic floor.

Patara
I think Patara could well be ripe for major development. But thankfully not yet. The beach is the big draw. There's 12 miles of it and it's fine, pale sand backed by sand dunes.

There is no natural shade on the beach but there are a couple of places for drinks and food. It's designated a Natural Park area so there's a ban – at least for the moment – on building between the beach and the ancient ruins. Accommodation is a mile or so behind the beach and many rooms are up in the foothills of the Taurus mountains. Some of these hillsides can be difficult to negotiate with a pushchair or walking stick.

Nightlife in Patara, as yet, is sociable but very quiet and relaxed. Patara is the birthplace of the Bishop of Myra, who was known for his kindness and generosity. After his death he was canonised as St Nicholas – and over the years he evolved into Santa Claus. Behind the beach at Patara you can see the remains of a triple arched gate, built around the first century AD, and a well-preserved theatre from the second century.

According to the companies selling holidays to Patara, the transfer time from Dalaman airport is either two and a half or three and a half hours.

Kalkan

Kalkan is a small and picturesque seaside village at the foot of wooded mountains. There are no beaches in Kalkan, which is probably why it hasn't developed faster. There are *dolmus* services and boats to the nearest beaches.

Patara, with its long sandy beach is about half an hour away by road, and Kapitas beach, between Kalkan and Kaş, is ten to fifteen minutes away on the road (or, more fun, by sea). From the road there's a long concrete stairway down to this deservedly popular sandy beach.

In Kalkan itself there is simple and usually new holiday accommodation, rooftop bars overlooking the bay, restaurants and some shops. You can take a local boat round to some of the many secluded bays on this stretch of the coast and to some nearby caves. You can also hop over by boat from the harbour to some rock terraces for swimming. I'm told the clear dazzling waters round here are good for dolphin spotting.

Transfer time to Kalkan from Dalaman airport is about three hours.

Kaş

Another charming, pretty and popular town (or is it an overgrown village?) on a bay at the foot of the Taurus mountains. There are white-painted houses, palm trees on the prom, a town square, bars and restaurants, shops and – like everywhere around this Lycian coast – a fair scattering of ancient remains.

There's only a pebbly beach in Kaş. The sandy beaches are a boat trip or a bumpy *dolmus* ride away. It's ten miles to the sandy beach of Kapitas (where there's no natural shade). The Greek island of Kastellorizon (Meis in Turkish) is two miles across the water. A popular boat trip is the three-hour ride over the clear blue water to the little island of Kekova with ancient remains under the sea.

Kaş was once ancient Antiphellos. You can visit the well-preserved ancient theatre and climb to the top for glorious views over the bay. There are remains of the ancient town walls near the shore and some Lycian tombs in the rock to the north-east of Kaş town.

The town of Demre, about 30 miles along the coast from Kaş, is close to the ancient city of Myra, where St Nicholas (Santa Claus) was bishop. There's a statue of Father Christmas and an annual festival is held there in early December to commemorate him.

Transfer time to Kaş from Dalaman airport is around three and a half hours.

Cavus

You won't find Cavus on any map yet. Only one tour operator is sending people there (Sunmed in 1989) so it's one place you can still take a package holiday and stay in uncommercialised Turkey. Not that there aren't places to eat and drink and a shop. You can hire a push bike. Accommodation is basic.

Transfer time from Antalya is two hours.

Kemer
Surprise, surprise! Kemer is actually a Turkish holiday resort that has been purpose-built to a government plan. The setting is as lovely as any along this stretch of the coast. The amenities are of a good standard and the major international holiday villages (Club Med, Club Robinson, Holiday Club International) all have developments here.

There's a new marina and high-class shopping, for designer leathers and so on. The town beach is pebbles and the other beaches nearby are shingle, pebbles and sand. Because it's a purpose-built and developing resort, Kemer is high on amenities and low on authentic Turkish charm. The concrete mixer count is higher than the donkey count.

Transfer time from Antalya airport is around one hour.

Beldibi
Beldibi hasn't yet been exploited by the British tour operators. It's about ten miles from Kemer, which is where you'd need to travel for shopping for all but the basics, and for a reasonable choice of nightlife. As in most places along this Lycian coast, the Taurus mountains drop down to the sea. The long beach is shingle, pebbles and sand.

Transfer time is 45 minutes from Antalya airport.

Antalya
Antalya is a major modern commercial city with a population of 250,000. There are beaches either side of the centre. Knoyaalti to the west is a four-mile stretch of pebbles with tatty cafes. Lara, a *dolmus* ride about seven miles to the east, is sandy, with holiday hotels, and therefore more crowded. The old part of Antalya city is a protected conservation area. Other sights to see are the picturesque old harbour, the bazaar and an imposing fluted minaret. There's also a well-preserved Hadrian's Gate, built in honour of his visit in AD 130, and a large, well laid out archaeological museum.

As Antalya is such a large and popular city, there's no shortage of places to eat, drink or shop. It's a pleasant place to explore and it makes a good central base for visiting the region, rather than a resort for a sun and beach holiday. Among the sites that are easy to visit from Antalya are Side, Termessos, Perge, Aspendos and, by boat, the spectacular waterfalls at Düden. You can buy tours to the sites in the city itself, or go it alone using a *dolmus*.

Antalya airport is outside the city.

Side

Side has a small, very busy, traffic-free centre that lies between two large beaches (coarse sand). Strictly speaking, the centre is called Selimiye but everyone now calls it Side. Until 1988 it was a holiday resort for Germans and weekending Turks. There are impressive ruins around the town including a grand Roman theatre.

Near the centre there are simple small hotels with gardens, many built in traditional Turkish style with pine shutters. The larger, more modern hotels are strung along the beaches. Plenty of places to eat and drink as well as shops for souvenirs and more serious shopping for carpets, leathers and jewellery. The town is always busy and full of day-trippers who've come to see the classical sights. As a result a lot of the eating places offer easy "international" food, so you need to shop around for a genuine Turkish feast. Many locals come to Side at weekends and on public holidays. Watersports, car hire and moped hire are available.

This area of the coast originally prospered because it was both a pirate's hang-out and it had a thriving slave market. The Romans developed the place into a wealthy city and it's the remains of their grand buildings that draw the tourists today. There's an impressive Roman theatre that was built to seat between 15,000 and 20,000 people, and a small museum on the site of the Roman baths. You can follow the colonnaded streets to the shore and the temple of the moon god. It's said that Mark Antony and Cleopatra took their holidays here. At the end of the 19th century, the Turks who left Crete settled here among the ruins. It's their descendants who are doing so well today in the Side tourism business.

Side is about one hour from Antalya airport.

Alanya

Alanya, the old town, juts out into the sea on a cliff with sweeping sandy beaches on either side. Alanya, the resort, is developing at the rate of one thousand new holiday beds a year, mostly along the coast road – a run of scruffy camp sites, concrete mixers and hotels. You can catch taxis, *dolmus* and buses at the gates of the main hotels to take you into town.

The climate is sub-tropical so you can see lush fruit orchards and banana plantations in the low foothills of the mountains. In high summer everything above the natural waterline is dry and arid. The old town has an impressive castle fortress and a busy commercial harbour. A famous landmark is a massive restored red-brick and stone octagonal tower built in AD 1225 to help protect the dockyard. It's now a museum. At the end of the west beach there's a cave with stalagmites almost fifty feet high. The cave's constant temperature of 72 degrees (22 Celsius) and 95 per cent humidity is supposed to bring relief to asthma sufferers.

Alanya has plenty of places for eating, drinking, shopping and noisy nightlife. From the harbour you can take boat trips to nearby caves, each with a well turned story to keep us happy. Pirates were supposed to have kept captured virgins in Maidens' Cave. The story you hear about Lovers' Cave depends on which holiday rep is telling the tale.

The town was a pirate haunt until the Romans took over. Mark Antony gave the area to Cleopatra as a present, so she could use the forest timber for building her barges and ships for the Egyptian navy. The classic sites of Side, Aspendos and Perge are easy day trips, as is an excursion eastwards along the spectacular coast to the Crusader castle at Anamur.

Transfer time to Alanya from Antalya airport is about two hours.

CHAPTER ELEVEN: EXCURSIONS

Turkey is littered with important relics and remains of great ancient civilisations. The country is almost one great outdoor museum, full of tombs and monuments, fancy columns, imposing arches and enormous outdoor theatres. Everywhere there's evidence of the different peoples who made their mark on the area – Greeks, Romans, Byzantines, Ottomans. All this *and* two of the ancient wonders of the world. Wherever you're holidaying in Turkey, you won't be far from some interesting ancient site, set in delightfully pretty countryside. Even those of us who slept through history at school can't fail to be impressed by the sheer size and importance of some of these places.

Because Turkey is so new to mass tourism and because there are so many ancient relics lying around, there haven't been the funds to investigate thoroughly and organise many of the "second division" sites. Most of these are gloriously undisturbed and uncommercialised. In many places you can still rest on some fallen marble column, there'll be bits of mosaic floor under the dust beneath your feet and you'll share the peace, the wonderful view and the ruins with a passing farmer and a few goats.

The more famous sites feature in organised tours that you can buy through your holiday company rep or through a local tour company. Or of course you can visit them under your own steam. In an organised day trip you should have some sort of English-speaking guide. Some are excellent and really bring the history of the place alive. Others can be dreadful: they either can't speak understandable English or they trot out the flimsiest of "historical" stories to keep their punters interested until lunch or the coach stop for a swim. One guide I followed offered four different stories as to the origin of some ancient minor league ruin. I asked him which version was most likely to be accurate. He said he hadn't a clue. He just came out with stories that sounded interesting. For a raki-inspired dare, I made up a fifth tale of the "truly authentic historical" story behind a certain feature. I have to report that he's still churning it out every trip.

Here's an authentic guide to the "first division" sites that the holiday companies feature as excursions. They're listed in geographical order, working down the coast from the North. If you're interested in this sort of sightseeing, the list might help influence your choice of holiday resort. Serious history buffs will want to take a much more detailed archaeological guide book to the sites. Buy your book before you leave home. You can buy books at the major sites like Ephesus, but the translation and quality of pictures can leave a lot to be desired.

You need to take comfortable walking shoes, plenty of film for the camera and a hat, sunscreen and a bottle of water (well, something liquid) for the heat.

Çanakkale and Gallipoli

The town of Çanakkale is about a six-hour bus ride from Istanbul (195 miles) or Izmir (200 miles). It's not a holiday resort but it's a well visited centre. It lies on the Dardanelles, the straits that link the Aegean to the Sea of Marmaris and thus the Black Sea. On the other side of the Dardanelles is the narrow peninsula of Gelibolu or Gallipoli – a name synonymous with the senseless slaughter of troops in the First World War.

Germans, Australians and New Zealanders in particular come to see the battlefield where, in one day, one third of the Allied fleet was wiped out trying to force a passage for supplies through the straits. After a campaign of five months, the final toll of casualties was a quarter of a million on each side. There's now a war museum at Çanakkale, as well as monuments to the Turkish, British and French dead at Seddulbahir and to the Australians and New Zealanders at Ariburnu. In August the Turks hold a Troy festival at Çanakkale.

Troy

Troy itself is twenty miles south of Çanakkale and five thousand years away in history and legend. The ancient city was strategically sited on a hill overlooking the plains and just south of where the Aegean meets the Dardanelles. In fact there were nine different cities built on this site over the centuries, which makes for confusing excavations, although they are labelled to show which layer is which Troy. The first city was built between 3000 and 2500 BC. There's an archaeological museum containing finds from the region near Çanakkale. To many visitors the most interesting bit is the huge wooden horse. OK, so it's a replica but it makes a great snapshot.

Serious students of the myths, legends and ancient history of Troy read a translation of Homer's *Iliad* for his account of the Trojan War. That's the one which started when Paris, son of the king of Troy, was offered the most beautiful woman in the world by the goddess Aphrodite. That turned out to be Helen, who had the unfortunate face that launched a thousand ships. Paris kidnapped her from Greece and carried her home to Troy, pursued by her old man Menelaus, his brother Agamemnon and a mighty Greek army. The seige of Troy dragged on for nine years, with starring roles played by such heroes as Achilles, Ajax and Odysseus, until finally the Greeks captured the city by the crafty subterfuge of the hollow wooden horse. Or so the story goes.

If you want to see the site of the judgement of Paris – where the young man picked Aphrodite as winner in a sort of goddesses' beauty contest and so started all the trouble – you need to travel further South to Mount Ida, now known as Kaz Daği.

Pergamon

The modern city of Bergama is a 60-mile drive (one and a half hours) from Izmir through fertile and picturesque countryside. The ancient town of Pergamon was once the capital of one of the most powerful kingdoms in Asia Minor. Today's site is enormous. It covers 30,000 acres but there are buses and taxis you can catch between the different areas. Even so, stiletto heels and flipflops won't work. There's a good deal of difficult ground to cover here.

The place started as a small settlement around the fourth century BC but it grew into a major centre of learning, art and medicine. Most of the old Greek city is on the slopes and summit of a hill – worth the climb for the views. There's a steep 15,000-seat theatre, a palace, barracks, temples and a notable library that once held 200,000 books. This is where parchment was invented: when the Egyptians banned the export of their papyrus, the scribes of Pergamon turned to using sheepskins and goatskins to write on. The celebrated library of books, by the way, ended up in Alexandria because Mark Antony gave the collection to Cleopatra.

The Asklepieion is another area to visit. Here is the Sanctuary of Asklepios, the god of healing, where doctors and philosophers came up with the concepts of herbal medicine, water and mud baths, blood transfusions, the power of positive thinking and the analysis of dreams – to name just some of their subjects of investigation.

There was once an astonishingly ornate Altar of Zeus here but if you want to see it you need to take another holiday – to East Berlin. It's now in the Pergamon museum there. In Bergama there are two museums, cafes and the Red Courtyard, a first century AD temple, later converted into a Byzantine basilica. In June there's a folklore festival in Bergama.

Sardis

Sardis is 60 miles east of Izmir and an easy day trip. The tour companies often combine the Izmir-Sardis excursion with a visit to Manisa, a country market town with some interesting mosques.

Sardis has a colourful history even if there isn't much to see. It used to be the capital of the ancient kingdom of Lydia and it was a pretty rich place. Its wealth came from trade with the East and from gold found in the river Paktolos. One theory is that they would dredge the gold from the river in oiled sheepskins – and from that came the legend of the Golden Fleece.

The last ruler of Sardis is the most famous: King Croesus. He reigned in the sixth century BC but was knocked off his throne by the Persians who captured Sardis and all its wealth. They in turn were defeated by Alexander the Great of Macedon in 334 BC. Sardis, by the way, was the first place to dream up a system of metal coins – around 600 BC.

Today you can see a restored part of a marble paved road and the remains of the Temple of Artemis which was first built under orders from Croesus and was rebuilt during Alexander's reign as one of the largest Greek temples in the world. There are good views from the top of the acropolis hill, although the remains are scanty.

Ephesus

This is the big one: the one people travel for long hot hours to see and, in my experience, they always say that the journey was worth every dusty bump and lurch. From resorts in the south of Turkey, it's offered as a two-day, one-night trip.

Ephesus is 47 miles south of Izmir and 10 miles from the busy resort of Kuşadasi. The place gets very crowded with tour groups. If you're planning to see it independently, the quietest times are usually first thing in the morning and very late in the afternoon. Do remember just how hot it can get at midday in summer.

There are four main areas to visit in Ephesus: the site of the temple of Artemis – once one of the ancient wonders of the world – the Virgin Mary's house, the grotto of the seven sleepers and Ephesus City.

Delightfully Turkish: nuts, dried fruits, spices, honey and sticky sweets.

There have been Lydian, Greek, Roman and Byzantine cities on this site. Ephesus was already a flourishing city when it was captured by King Croesus around 550 BC; later, when he was booted out, Ephesus came under Persian rule. Around the 400s it became the headquarters of the Spartan general Lysander, then went back to the Persians until Alexander the Great marched in, in 334 BC. The city at that time was set around the Temple of Artemis but was then moved nearer to the sea. In those days the water came much further inland than today. That old inlet and harbour area later silted up.

The Romans ruled the city from 133 BC. They made Ephesus the capital of their province of Asia and it was the second largest city in the East after Alexandria. It was seriously damaged by an earthquake in AD 29, but the emperor Hadrian later organised important engineering works around the harbour. The city declined in importance and power as the harbour gradually silted up.

Of all the magnificent streets, squares, houses, mosaics and buildings to see, the centrepiece at Ephesus has to be the Great Theatre which seats 25,000. Building started on it during the reign of Claudius (AD 41-54). It's in an excellent state of preservation and needless to say the finest views of the whole area are from the top of the theatre. It's worth the climb. This must be the only theatre where you feel that the expression "a seat in the gods" takes on an almost literal meaning. And yes, you guessed it, Cleopatra came here to meet Mark Antony. You can test the excellent acoustics of the theatre (a few lines from the *Iliad* perhaps?).

St Paul preached in the theatre, causing the riot of the silversmiths (read all about it: Acts 19 verses 23-41). The local silversmiths in those days made comfortable livings selling silver statuettes of the goddess Artemis to visitors to her temple. They were understandably worried that if St Paul converted everyone to Christianity, they'd lose all their business. Hence the riot. In summer, shows are occasionally held in the theatre.

You can see various statues of Artemis in the well-organised museum at Selçuk, the modern Ephesus town. She's the goddess with rows of breasts – a symbol of fertility. Today there's just one column left of her temple, that wonder of the ancient world.

About five miles from Ephesus is the house where the Virgin Mary is said to have lived out her last days at what is now called Meryemana. She went to Ephesus with St John and in the late nineteenth century a German nun had a vision of Mary in her house. A small cottage was found here that perfectly fitted the vision. A chapel to the Virgin was built on the spot and this century it has been visited by both Pope Paul IV in 1967 and Pope John Paul II in 1980. Every August 15 on the Feast of the Assumption, a special commemoration service is held here.

The cave of the seven sleepers has a touching story to it. Seven young Christian lads and their dog had to flee the town in the third century because they were being persecuted for their faith. They hid in this cave in the hillside. One story goes that when they woke up one of them went back to the town to buy bread. He tried to pay with outdated coins and it dawned on everyone that the boys had been asleep for two hundred years. By then Ephesus was a Christian city and they were welcomed back with open arms. Other tales tell of an earthquake opening up the cave and the boys being discovered alive. The cave became a shrine.

Keen historians and amateur archaeologists can happily spend days visiting and studying the sites here. Most tourists whip round in about three hours. The monuments are labelled and you can buy booklets on the site.

Turkish trivial pursuits
Learning that the temple at Ephesus is one of the ancient wonders of the world always prompts the question: what are the other six? I've never met anyone who could name them off the top of their head. Here's your chance to win a bottle of raki from your fellow travellers. The seven ancient wonders of the world are:

- The temple of Artemis (Diana) at Ephesus
- The Mausoleum at Halikarnassus (now Bodrum)
- The Pyramids of Egypt
- The Hanging Gardens of Babylon
- The Colossus at Rhodes
- The statue of Jupiter at Olympia
- The Pharos (lighthouse) of Alexandria.

(The Great Wall of China and the Taj Mahal are considered to be contenders for the list of wonders of the *modern* world. If it's a long coach journey, you could try to agree on a final list for seven modern wonders.)

Aphrodisias

Aphrodisias is usually coupled with Pamukkale as a very long day's excursion from Kuşadasi (a 320-mile round trip), or as a two-day, one-night trip from resorts further south. Aphrodisias is inland around 90 miles east of Kuşadasi. The drive alone is a treat. The fertile countryside around here is full of orchards and crops.

In the second century BC Aphrodisias was a notable centre of art and culture dedicated to the goddess of love Aphrodite (Venus). An earthquake in 1958 caused the locals to evacuate the area, leaving it clear for major excavations.

The local museum is full of statues of the goddess – all surprisingly modest, considering her role in life. The sights include a lovely white stone theatre, baths and a temple dedicated to Aphrodite of course. There's also a spectacular and well-preserved stadium built for games and chariot races, with seats for 30,000 people.

Pamukkale

Pamukkale is at the top of any list of great natural wonders of Turkey. This steep hillside of petrified waterfalls is a fascinating place. Pamukkale means "cotton castle", so called because these strange and wondrous white deposits are supposed to look like edifices of raw cotton. There are stalactites and pools overflowing with warm water (at 95 degrees Fahrenheit) and ancient remains are littered around the place.

People have been visiting the area since ancient times, mainly for the healing powers of the natural warm springs. There's probably been a town here since 190 BC. The centre used to be called Hierapolis and it flourished as a spa, as a tourist spot and as the centre of a thriving wool industry. If you visit the motels here you can still swim in the warm waters. There's a 10,000-seat Roman theatre to see, enormous Roman baths and the remains of an arcaded street. There are also burial grounds with stone sarcophagi and chamber tombs (for those who took the cure too late, perhaps).

Priene

Priene, Miletus and Didyma are usually offered as one organised trip because they are close together. The sites are about 105 miles south of Izmir and around half-way between Ephesus and Bodrum. Again, the trip is almost worth the time just for the ride through the rural scenery. By the way, those small blue "shoe-boxes" you might see in clusters on the hillsides are beehives.

Priene is set up on a hill overlooking what was the river Meander (Menderes) and is now green flat farmland. It was the sudden silting of the river in the eighth century AD that caused the decline of Priene and Miletus. Priene wasn't as large or as important as Miletus, but it was one of the first Greek cities to be built with proper town planning. You might just be able to make out its original grid system. Many of the ruins you see at Priene are 2000 years or so old. There's a small theatre. The *pièce de resistance* today is a row of five grand fluted columns. They're a photographer's dream.

Miletus

Fourteen miles to the south of Priene, Miletus was a much richer, more commercial city, whose citizens were good at venturing forth and colonising. They colonised some eighty places around the Black Sea, in the Aegean and in Egypt. What's left of the city is pretty scanty. An enormous Market Gate is in East Berlin. You can still see the city's Roman theatre that once held an audience of 25,000.

Didyma

Didyma is twelve miles south of Miletus and just three miles from the holiday resort of Altinkum (see page 93). In its heyday Didyma had a hugely important oracle with a reputation second only to the oracle at Delphi. The chosen mystic would sit on a tripod in a trance and come up with answers put to her by the country's most powerful rulers. Today I suppose such people have to consult their computer or their horoscope.

In 300 BC plans were laid to build a temple to Apollo – not just any temple but the biggest in the world. Over 150 years were spent on the building of this temple and they never did get round to finishing it. What's left is still impressive, though, and at the entrance to the site you can see a mighty stone head of Medusa that was once part of the temple's frieze.

Bodrum

For most day-trippers Bodrum is as much a shopping, eating and posing experience as an archaeological expedition. Bodrum may be one of the leading and liveliest holiday resorts on the coast but it also has its fair share of notable and grand history.

Bodrum used to be known as Halikarnassus, a town founded in 1200 BC by Dorian Greeks. With its good harbours and fertile land, it became a prosperous city. It came under Lydian rule in the reign of the rich King Croesus, then he lost it to the Persians. The Romans took over in 129 BC. In AD 395 Bodrum became part of the Byzantine Empire and in 1402 the Knights Hospitallers of St John invaded and built their castle.

During the Persians' reign there were many rulers (a fair number of them women) and the most famous was

Mausolus. He was supposed to have been a skilled statesman and during his time he had city walls, temples and harbours built in Bodrum. His wife (who was also his sister) succeeded him and completed his memorial – a monumental tomb. This was one of the seven wonders of the ancient world and from this tomb of Mausolus was coined the word *mausoleum*. Not a lot of people know that. (For a list of the other six wonders turn to page 117.)

There's little to see of the Mausoleum today. They reckon it stood 150 feet high, with a base 400 feet square. It had a pyramid shaped roof over thirty-six Ionic columns and a statue of a four-horse chariot on the very top. Its destruction was probably started by earthquakes and in 1402 the Knights used many of its rectangular stone blocks in the building of the castle. Many of the original sculptures from the tomb and from Bodrum castle are now in the British Museum. No wonder the Turks now have such strict laws banning the export of genuine antiques.

Bodrum's Castle of St Peter and its gardens is a marvellous crusader castle and a delight to visit as long as you're not there with too many crowds. The castle is Bodrum's major landmark, built between the two bays. The west bay, by the way, was the ancient naval harbour. As was the custom in the Crusader days, knights of different nationalities built the castle and each put up their own tower. These are still known as the English, French, Italian and German towers. A fifth tower is called the snake tower. The English tower now has a minstrel and wench selling drinks to visitors to the sound of taped minstrel Muzak!

In the castle you'll find the museum of underwater archaeology, full of artefacts found in shipwrecks around the coast. Fascinating stuff. Bodrum's most notable citizen was the Greek Herodotus, famous among classical scholars as the first European to use prose as the medium of a work of art. He travelled over a lot of the then known world, to Athens and through Egypt to Mesopotamia, Palestine and Southern Russia. He retired in Italy and penned the first straight history book.

For those who like twee stories, the mythical Fountain of Salmacis was supposed to have been sited along the west bay of Bodrum. The son of Hermes and Aphrodite fell in love with Salmacis. When he went to bathe in her water he became a hermaphrodite, half man and half woman. Grief-stricken – well you would be, wouldn't you? – he made his parents bewitch the water so that every man who dipped into it then lost his manly vigour. Looking around the bars and clubs of Bodrum of an evening, it's safe to say that this spell is no longer working.

On the hillside behind the Mausoleum there's a 10,000-seat theatre built by Mausolus which is still occasionally used today. See also Resort Reports, page 94.

Dalyan and Caunos

Dalyan village and the ruins at Caunos are about a 45-minute drive from Dalaman airport and around 60 miles east of Marmaris. A day-trip to see the tombs at Caunos is surely one of the most pleasant excursions you can take along the Mediterranean coast. The scenery around the area is lovely. To see these tombs that were carved into the high cliffsides probably in the fourth century BC, you really have to take a small boat along the river which connects Lake Köyceğiz (about seven by three miles in size) with the sea.

Dalyan is a little town on the river between the lake and the sea. It's where the fish come to spawn and it now has a thriving fish farming industry. Cotton and vegetables are grown in the surrounding fields. Years ago the inhabitants of the whole area were wiped out by malaria. Happily, the disease is long gone from this part of Turkey.

There are restaurants and cafes by the waterside at Dalyan and it's by the grace of the gods and the force of vocal conservationists that there isn't a huge holiday hotel on the beach here. There were expensive plans for one – you can see why: it's such an idylic spot – but Dalyan is one of the very, very few places left on the Mediterranean where loggerhead turtles come to lay their eggs. Tourists might like sharing the beach with hundreds of other humans. Turtles do not. Happily, permission to build a major international hotel was withdrawn at the eleventh hour.

The trip in a small boat up the river to the lake is a delight. One hotel advertises the trip as "a sail through bamboo labyrinths not toutched (*sic*) by tourism until now". Most holiday reps call the boat they use the African Queen. The river and the lake don't look much like Africa, but I have heard fellow passengers liken the area to both the Norfolk Broads and Thailand. There's plenty of interesting birdlife around this area. I'm no ornithologist but I did spot cranes overhead and a kingfisher diving into the water from the reeds. The theatrical-looking tombs are impressive.

Nearby you can scramble up a rocky hillside to see the remains of an ancient theatre and an acropolis. It was here in 1985 that a knowledgeable tourist discovered a mosaic floor under the sand. He came back soon after with another expert, only to discover that some souvenir hunter had beaten him to it and lifted it. There are also warm sulphur baths with mud that's supposed to be good for you when you plaster it all over your body. It smells so foul it *must* be doing you good.

Xanthos and Letoon

There are a lot of stones to see in Xanthos. In places you see the farmers trying to plough round elaborately carved bits of marble columns. Xanthos is set back off the main road by the village of Kinik between Fethiye and Kalkan, in pine forest country. The site is on a hill about five miles back from the sea. Xanthos used to be the main city of Lycia, which is sometimes called "the oldest republic in the world". There were twenty cities in this republic and they were governed by a popular assembly and a president. No-one is sure about the origin of the Lycians except that they weren't Greek and that they originally had an Indo-European language which was later written with the Greek alphabet.

In 545 BC the Persians destroyed Xanthos. In 333 BC Alexander the Great captured the rebuilt city. The Seleucids ruled it in the third century and Rhodes took over in 188 BC.

The Romans helped the citizens fight off the Rhodians. One story told by the local guides tells of Brutus laying siege to the city to force the citizens to pay taxes to support the war with Antony and Cleopatra. The Xanthion men instead burned their women and children and killed themselves. Brutus wept.

Xanthos is famous for its Lycian pillar-tombs which were put up between the sixth and fourth centuries BC. You can see the old Lycian inscriptions on some of the stones. There's also a Roman theatre that would once have seated 10,000. At the top of the theatre is the Tomb of the Harpies, with delightful marble carvings of these creatures who were half woman, half animal.

In the mid-nineteenth century a British party started to excavate the site and many of the marble carvings and statues from here were shipped back to the British Museum.

Three miles south is Letoon, once an important sanctuary. Remains have been found here of temples dedicated to Leto, Artemis and Apollo. Leto was loved by Zeus and she had two children, Apollo and Artemis. She was washing them one day, so the story goes, when she was driven away by local shepherds. She wasn't too happy with this behaviour so as a punishment she turned them into frogs. The wolves helped Leto to survive and in gratitude she named the land Lycia after the Greek word *lykos* – "wolf".

Kaş

The modern bustling resort of Kaş, on the southern tip of Lycia, is sited on what was once ancient Antiphellos. There are some impressive Lycian rock tombs which were probably built some time during the fourth century BC. There's a necropolis containing a tomb decorated with carvings of children holding hands and dancing. There's also a fine sarcophagus by the quayside, and a well preserved ancient theatre.

(See also the Kaş resort report on page 104.)

Kekova
Boat trips to the sunken city at Kekova are deservedly popular excursions. The scenery along the coastline alone is worth the trip. The best way to glimpse the ruins of the sunken city is with a snorkel and face mask, swimming from the excursion boat.

Myra and Demre
There's nothing special to look at in Demre (25 miles east of Kaş) except a lovely eleventh-century Byzantine basilica that covers the tomb of St Nicholas and a park that has a statue of Santa Claus! This is because St Nicholas of Myra, who was born in Patara around AD 300 and became the bishop of Myra, was buried here. Some stories say that this St Nicholas, being a generous fellow; would drop anonymous gifts of money down the chimneys of poor families. Other tales tell of him throwing the money through the windows of three women who had told the bishop that without dowries they would have to become prostitutes. You get the gist. St Nicholas's feast day, December 6th, became associated with present giving. The saint somehow acquired a white beard, a red cloak and a sackful of toys, and most people who don't holiday around here carry on thinking he was born by the North Pole. Most of his bones were stolen by Italians in 1087 and taken to a basilica in Bari, Italy. The few bones that the thieves left are in the museum at Antalya.

Demre is built around the ancient Lycian city of Myra. St Paul visited the place in AD 61 on his first journey to Rome. There are many impressive rock tombs on the hillside and a large Roman theatre with the usual impressive litter of old rocks and chunks of columns.

Aspendos
The site of Aspendos is 30 miles from Antalya and about nine miles inland from the coast against a backdrop of mountains. The impressive theatre you see today was built

by the Romans but Aspendos the town dates back to at least 1000 BC when it was built on what were the banks of the River Eurymedon.

Aspendos was a prosperous river port as in olden times the river was navigable from the coast. Today there's the most impressive Roman theatre to visit and sit in. It's now recognised as the largest and best preserved in Asia Minor. It was built in the second century AD by the Curtius brothers and could hold an audience of up to 20,000. There are thirty-nine tiers of seats and, running round the theatre at the top, a wonderful barrel-vaulted colonnade. There are also a few remains of an ancient aquaduct and water towers, and a hilltop acropolis.

Perge
Perge is eleven miles north-east of Antalya and is an ancient Greek town where St Paul once preached. Like many of the places along the coast, Perge went into decline when the nearby harbour silted up. Maths wizards should note that Perge was the birthplace of Apollonios (born 262 BC) who was a pioneering geometrician. The Romans took Perge in 188 BC. The town's temple of Artemis was once considered as important as the one at Ephesus until it was plundered by Artemidoros around 80 BC.

Perge is reputed to have had one of the oldest Christian communities in Asia Minor. Some people claim that St Paul preached his first sermons here. Of course, there's a theatre. It was built in the third century AD and it's a 15,000-seater. From the top of it you can see across to the well-preserved games stadium. There's also a huge entrance gate, Roman baths and a photogenic colonnaded street, as well as mosaic floors by an agora.

Termessos
Termessos is up in the hills 20 miles north-west of Antalya at the foot of the ancient Mount Solmos (today's Gulluk Daği). It's a hard climb along a mountain road and then by foot to the summit. The origins of the town are lost in the

mists of time. The remains you see today date from the second and third centuries AD. The views over the Gulf of Antalya and the crisper mountain air are worth the effort of getting there. There are remains of a Roman theatre, gymnasium, temples and tombs.

Not far away along the road is the Karain Cave – the oldest inhabited cave that has yet been found in the country. Learned evidence shows that this cosy homestead was inhabited back in the Paleolithic Age – 50,000 years ago. The tools, flints and skeletons found round here are now in the museum at Antalya.

Side

Side offers the best of both worlds. It's a busy, lively and deservedly popular beach resort built around impressive and important classical antiquities. There was a settlement on this pretty peninsula back in 1000 BC. The inhabitants made the bay into a safe harbour and became proficient sailors. It then became something of a pirate's den with a thriving slave market. The Romans moved in, cleaned the place up and put up impressive buildings, some of which you can still see today. It was the silting up of the harbour and raids by Arabs that led to the collapse of Side as a prosperous city.

Today's prospering inhabitants come from Crete and settled here around the beginning of this century. They now mainly make their money, not from piracy or slaves, but from holidaymakers. The name Side probably means "pomegranate" in some ancient Anatolian language. Romantics always tell you that it was in Side that Mark Antony and Cleopatra enjoyed a loving holiday. There's a great Roman gate at the end of two colonnaded streets. One of the streets leads to a colonnaded square. There's a large, well-preserved Roman theatre that held up to 15,000 in 49 rows of seating.

The two major temples both have remains to see. They were probably dedicated to Athena and Apollo. The Roman baths have been rebuilt and made into a museum which is decorated with statues and sculptures from the area. A tour through the rooms shows you how the rich Romans liked to bathe: first the *frigidarium* – the cold room – for undressing. Then the hot room – *caldarium* – warmed by an underfloor heating system. Then into the steam room – *laconicum* – before starting the cool-down process in the warm room – *tepidarium*. (See also the resort report on Side on page 106.)

Manavgat
Not far from Side you can visit the little waterfalls across the River Manavgat, which in ancient times was called the River Melas. There are places for food and drinks by the waterfalls.

CHAPTER TWELVE: MESSING ABOUT IN BOATS

You can't holiday on the Turkish coast without taking to the water, even if it's only for one half-day trip. A boat trip is the best way to appreciate just how stunning the Turkish shoreline can be – especially from around Bodrum and down along the Mediterranean coast. Those staggering hills with their swathes of pine trees and thyme bushes are the stuff poems and paintings are made of. And the sea water is everything you want it to be: clear turquoise, velvet blue, wine dark. For once you can't accuse the travel brochures of taking poetic liberties. And a sailing holiday in Turkey should cost you about £1000 *less* than a sail in the Caribbean.

I'm scared of water. I don't like swimming out of my depth and I'm prone to seasickness. Hardly a candidate for a cruise on Turkish seas. Yet even I enjoy sweeping rather majestically over these waters. It's true that I'm more likely to be holding a glass than a snorkel but even I've been known to get my swimming costume wet. Those waters are very tempting. And during my cruising days, the only time I felt unwell, I have to blame my queasiness on the brandy, not the waves.

Sailing for landlubbers
For non-sailors, there's one magnificent way of sailing the seas and exploring the Turkish coastline: book a week on a *gulet*. A gulet (usually pronounced sort of goo-let) is a typically Turkish wooden sailing boat around fifteen to

twenty metres long. You'll see them lined up in the harbours and marinas along the coast, especially at Bodrum and Marmaris. Gulets are attractive to look at, although they are motorised and most of their "sailing" is powered by the boat's engine. The sails are often just to please the photographers. Passengers don't have to know anything about nautical matters. There's a Turkish crew of two or three on each gulet who sail the boat, cook your meals *and* do the washing up.

In theory, the passengers chart the route or at least say where they want to go. In practice, because a weekly charter has to have a set starting and finishing point and time, the route is pretty well mapped out for you. You potter along from bay to bay, harbour to harbour. The gulets that the holiday companies use usually take from six to twelve passengers. They're built with tiny double cabins, toilets and showers. Up above, there's a sundeck and a shaded lounge/dining area at the stern. In my experience, the food served is simple but fresh and filling. Supper might well include fish caught that morning by the "captain". Usually the price of the holiday includes the meals on board. You just pay for drinks and for any meals you eat in restaurants off the boat. Dress on board is always informal. A gulet is not the QE2. Dressing for dinner means putting on a dry T-shirt and a liberal coating of insect repellant.

During the week's cruise there are chances to moor at resorts and near archaeological sites. You also get to swim in the idyllic bays and coves that can't be reached by road. These days, however, some of the prettiest bays are on every boat's itinerary and in some of them you may even have to queue up for your "spontaneous" beach barbecue. But in a bay that hasn't got any *locanta* or beach bar yet, you'll almost certainly have the place to yourself once the daytrippers have sailed for home. There are steps from the boat into the water for those (like me) who can't dive and are too wimpish to jump in. But once you're in, I promise you, the water's wonderful.

Most gulets have their own sound system and cassette

player. Take your own tapes if you're fussy about what you listen to. Obviously, if enough of you on board want peace and quiet, you can order it. Then you just have to keep away from the ravers on the other boats.

Possible snags

The cabins are small and can get very stuffy (especially if you're next to the loo). I couldn't sleep in mine. Instead every night I crashed out with some blankets on a sunbathing mattress up on deck. Peeping round the blankets at dawn in the fresh sea air and watching the sun rise and feeling the air warm up is wonderful. It's also an excellent cure for a Turkish hangover.

There's no escaping the other passengers. You might turn out to be like-minded spirits and end up lifelong friends. You might not. The obvious way round this is to travel with a group of friends you know well and charter the whole boat.

You may well need to use the section in this book on speaking Turkish. Some crews don't speak much English. If you think you'll want to make complicated requests of the crew, take along a full phrase book.

Day trips afloat

You can buy full-day and half-day boat trips at most holiday resorts. Many British travel companies also sell organised boat trips to their holidaymakers.

You chug along on motorised sailing boats to nearby islands or beaches, sometimes to parts of the coast that are inaccessible by road. You can usually buy cold drinks on board, and you'll doubtless be "entertained" by loud music from the skipper's cassette player. Sometimes lunch on board is included in the price – check when you buy the trip – at other times, you go ashore at a beach with a *lokanta*. Take plenty of suntan cream to sea with you.

Flotilla sailing

Not everyone is the water wimp I am. It's possible to

explore the Turkish waters without having a crew to do all the work. Flotilla sailing holidays on small yachts are organised by some companies and they seem to suit newish sailors who don't have the experience to sail off on their own. On a flotilla holiday a group of small yachts sail the same route following an experienced "lead" boat. The yachters meet up in the evenings and there's help on hand if you get into difficulties. This is real sailing – not the motorised pretend stuff of gulet cruises and you'll probably cover 120-200 nautical miles in a week. The winds in the south-west of Turkey are at their strongest in June, July, August and the beginning of September. If you know Greek waters, you'll find the Turkish summer winds stronger than those in the Ionian sea. (Read on for more information of the winds.)

The yachts used for flotilla sailing can be small enough for a couple, or three-cabin boats that take up to six passengers. Each yacht is equipped with bedding, and enough cutlery and crockery to make (simple) meals. Life on board is "intimate" and a fast, accurate way of testing a relationship. You usually need to take your own towels and a waterproof. You pay for your own food supplies and meals, but mooring charges are usually included in the holiday price.

A "villa flotilla" holiday offers a week on land and a week on the water. You can also buy land-based holidays that include tuition on sailing dinghies and yachts.

Bareboat charters

A bareboat charter is when you hire a boat for a week or more of independent sailing. In fact, if you need to have the expression explained, you aren't yet enough of a sailor to be allowed to take one. Companies ask for a "declaration of experience" when you book a bareboat charter, and they have the right not to let you sail it, if you turn up in Turkey having lied about your sailing prowess. I'm told that the boat people know as soon as you climb on board whether or not you know what you are doing. Mooring charges shouldn't break the bank. They're usually around £1 per night, payable in Turkish lire.

A possible risk pointed out to me by knowledgeable sailing operators: in the crowded, hottest months of July and August, water you take on board especially from the busy centres at Bodrum and Marmaris can be "bad". Don't drink it.

Winds to watch

On the central and southern Aegean in summer the winds normally blow from the north-west to the south-east. This wind is called the *meltem* although around Çeşme, Izmir and Kuşadasi it is known locally as the *imbat*.

In early and late summer the *meltem* blows less strongly and there are days of little or no wind. In high summer the *meltem* can blow very hot – rather like sailing through the stream of a hairdryer. Usually the *meltem* dies at night and resumes the next day around midday. It can occasionally blow day and night for days on end in the gulfs. The wind follows the coast to blow from the west and becomes weaker towards the head of the gulfs.

Gusts are particularly strong off the north coast of the Gulf of Gökova and the Gulf of Hisaronu. The *meltem* also blows in a westerly direction along the Mediterranean coast as far as the Gulf of Finike. Around the Gulf of Antalya there are both land and sea breezes. The sea breezes here blow mainly from the south and south-west. In the morning there will often be a land breeze blowing from the north. Winds in the spring and autumn are almost equally divided between north and south.

A meteorological bulletin in several languages is broadcast every day on the short wave band (25m) at 9.00, 12.00, 15.00 and 18.00 hours. The definitive Pilot Guide to the area has been written by Rod Heikell and is published by Imray, Laurie, Norie and Wilson. £17.50.

In Turkish waters

The Turkish Tourist Authority advises sailors that:

- International navigation rules should be scrupulously followed.
- The Turkish courtesy flag should be flown from 8 am to sunset.
- It is best to avoid zig-zagging between Turkish and Greek waters.
- Yachtsmen should strictly refrain from taking any "archaeological souvenirs" from the coastal waters and keeping them on board. The penalty is confiscation of the yacht.

Cruising

You can cruise along the coast in style on a grown-up cruise ship that stops for the day or half-day at the bigger ports and resorts for you to have a quick look round. The cruise ship organisers also bus you to the important archaeological sites. Some organise learned speakers on history and archaeology to accompany the group so you have your own tame boffin on hand. For many keen history buffs this kind of cruise offers a mix of "safe" and sometimes luxurious floating accommodation with a taste of Turkey during your excursions on land.

For information of the cruising and yachting holiday companies see chapter sixteen.

Board silly

As the tourists move in, so do the windsurf boards. If you're the sporting sort whose holiday will be ruined if you are not out in the water and up on a sailboard most days, you must check with the holiday company before you book that there will be boards for hire near where you're staying. The strong summer winds along the south-west corner of Turkey are good for experienced windsurfers. Novices will have the easiest time in October when the winds should drop. If you're a serious windsurfer, or you're keen to learn properly, look for a specialist holiday company that will have a stock of at least one and a half boards per would-be windsurfer – light wind boards and strong wind boards.

They should also offer English-speaking instructors with Royal Yachting Association qualifications.

Scuba-duby-doo?
Turkish water can be so clear it begs you to don face mask and snorkel. You can hire or buy masks and snorkels at the larger resorts. Pack your own if you have a set. Beware burning your back as you float around.

CHAPTER THIRTEEN:
BLUFF YOUR WAY
THROUGH TURKISH HISTORY

Even on the simplest lazing and lager holiday in Turkey you cannot help bumping into the most impressive evidence of the country's complicated and imposing history: a Roman arch here, a Greek stadium there and everywhere statues and portraits of a leader called Mustapha Kemel Atatürk.

The history of a small island like Britain is simplicity itself compared to that of Turkey's which involves too many different cultures, changing borders and overlapping civilisations ever to be presented in a simple, straightforward way.

However, here's a very oversimplified crib sheet for just some of the major names that you can't help hearing mentioned once you set foot in Turkey.

Way back when . . .
The very first recorded citizens in the land we now call Turkey were into wall paintings and pottery as long ago as 7500 BC. Evidence of their existence was found at Çatal Höyök in central Anatolia which, along with Jericho, is the oldest known settlement in the world.

The Hittites
The Hittites were around from the old bronze age (about 2600 BC) and 1000 years later they established their first kingdom. The Hittites went to war with the Egyptian Pharaohs, notably Ramesis II. You can see Hittite jewellery, pottery and ironwork in Ankara museum. The

Hittites gradually lost out to other invading civilisations.

The Lycians, Lydians and Phrygians
These were smaller civilisations that set up shop mainly around and along the Aegean and Mediterranean coasts. *King Midas* – the one with the golden touch, who reigned around 715 BC – is the most famous Phrygian. The Lycian kingdom spread from around Fethiye down to Antalya and the Lycians left behind the remarkable cliff-face tombs you can see in this area. The major king of the Lydian civilisation (680-547 BC) was another rich one, *Croesus*.

The Trojan War
For the tale of this legendary Greek expedition into the area, see Troy on page 111.

The Greeks
Ionians, Aeolians and Dorians from mainland Greece founded cities all along the Aegean coast from around 1000 BC onwards. Many of them became famous centres of culture and learning. For centuries, the Greeks had problems with . . .

The Persians
They came from the East to conquer and control the Anatolian region in the 6th century BC. Despite occasional revolts and rebellions by Greek city-states, much of the area was part of the Persian Empire – until Alexander the Great marched in and took over in 334 BC.

Alexander
The young and highly energetic king of Macedon first conquered mainland Greece, then headed east. He made short work of the region that's now Turkey, swept on into Egypt, then ploughed through the crumbling Persian Empire and even conquered territories in North India. When he died there at the age of 33, his general Seleucus assumed control of the Turkish bit of his empire.

The Seleucids
Seleucus' descendants managed to rule the area for nearly 200 years, with Pergamon as their capital. The later Seleucids made an alliance with the Romans, and when the last king died in 133 BC, he bequeathed his kingdom to Rome.

The Romans
In 129 BC they declared the western part of modern Turkey a Roman province, and called it Asia. The Romans brought bureaucracy, a stable government, grand buildings and roads. The conditions were also ideal for the spread of a brand-new world-class religion.

St Paul
He was born in Tarsus and in AD 47 travelled through Western Turkey (amongst other countries) preaching and converting people to Christianity. For two years he lived and preached in Ephesus where he caused a riot among the silversmiths. See page 115.

Byzantium
The Roman Emperor Constantine the Great made the city of Byzantium into the capital of the Empire in 330 AD and it was later named after him as Constantinople.

Emperor Justinian
Justinian, 527-565, is remembered as a good conqueror, winning back a lot of land including Italy and Egypt for the Eastern Empire. In Contantinople he ordered the building of the magnificent St Sophia which, a thousand years later, was turned into a mosque.

Mohammed
Mohammed was born in Mecca in 570. He became the Messenger of God reciting the Holy word of God to his fellow citizens. After his death these recitations were recorded in the Koran. Mohammed was forced to flee

Dolmabahçe Palace, Istanbul: sultans made it their residence in the nineteenth century and Atatürk died here in 1938.

Mecca because of his recitations in 622 and this year became the starting point for the Moslem lunar calendar.

Only fifty years later Moslems – followers of Islam – had conquered Persia, Egypt and the land between Mecca and Constantinople.

The Seljuk Turks
This is the first Turkish dynasty. The Seljuk Empire 1037-1109 covered most of today's Turkey as well as what is now known as Iraq and Iran. The poet Omar Khayyam ("The Moving Finger writes; and, having writ,/Moves on:") was a Seljuk. A small part of the empire survived for another 140 years or so in Anatolia producing Jelaleddin Rumi who founded the Whirling Dervish order.

The Ottoman Empire
What became the great Ottoman Empire was originally founded by Osman around 1288. This empire became powerful under . . .

Mehmet the Conqueror
In 1453 Mehmet captured Constantinople and put an end to the Byzantine Empire. He renamed the city Istanbul.

Sultan Süleyman the Magnificent
Süleyman (1520-1566) is also known as the Law Giver. He lead the empire through its most glorious period. He built more beautiful buildings in Istanbul and Jerusalem and expanded the empire as far as (but not including) Vienna.

His son was dubbed the "Sot" and decline set in after Süleyman's death.

Atatürk
You don't need to be a history buff to know of Mustafa Kemal Atatürk's existence, 1881-1938. His portrait is everywhere. Have a look round your hotel reception area. The Turkish people revere him (with good reason) and it is an offence to speak badly of him. I suggest you never do.

He was born in Macedonia when Turkey was ruled by weak and ineffective sultans. He was a good soldier and a member of the Young Turk movement. After World War 1, when Turkey fought against the Allies, he organised resistance to plans for Allied control and a Greek invasion.

Under his dynamic leadership the sultanate and the Ottoman Empire were finally abolished and on 29 October 1923 the Republic of Turkey was proclaimed with Mustafa Kemal as its first president.

He set about bringing Turkey into the twentieth century. The arabic alphabet was latinised. Polygamy was abolished. In 1934 women got the vote and the right to serve in parliament. Family names became compulsory. Until then moslims each had only one given name and Turks in 1935 were told to take a family name. Atatürk's name then was just Mustafa although he'd kept the nickname given to him at school which was Kemal meaning excellence. He chose his family name to be "Father Turk" – Atatürk. He also banned the wearing of the fez. (See pages 54 & 56.)

As I said, the Turkish people respect and are very grateful to Atatürk.

CHAPTER FOURTEEN: TALKING TURKISH

These days you can get by in the big holiday resorts without speaking any Turkish. Many of the locals are only too happy to try their English out on you.

In the smaller places, however, you can have problems communicating. Mind you, most holidaymakers can get by with much smiling and furious arm waving. If you know any German you'll find that a lot of Turks speak it as a second language.

Even so, it's fun to pick up a few words of Turkish and the people you try it on will warm to you immediately.

As a guide to pronunciation:

ö is the same as in German and a sort of "ur" as in Sir
ü is as in German and a sort of "ew" as in dew
c is said as "j" in job
ç sounds like "ch" as in church
g is hard as in good
ğ isn't said at all. Pretend it's not there
ş is said as "sh" as in shall
v is soft, nearly like w

hello	**merhaba**
good morning/day	**günaydin**
goodbye	**allaha ismarladik** (only said by the person who is leaving)
	güle güle (said by the person who stays)
yes	**evet**

Who needs to speak the language with translations as good as this?

no	hayir
please	lütfen
thank you	teşekkür ederim
thank you very much	çok teşekkür ederim
thanks	mersi
none	yok
much/very	çok
left	sol
right	sağ
good	iyi
bad	fenah
big	büyük
small	küçük
open	açik
closed	kapali
when?	ne zaman?
where?	nerede?
how?	nasil?
now/at present	şimdi
tomorrow	yarin
give me	. . . bana verin
I want	. . . istiyorum
where is the toilet?	tuvalet nerede?
it's very noisy	çok gürültülü
what does it cost?	kaç lira?
price	fiyat
cheaper	daha ucuz
very expensive	çok pahali
soap	sabun

towel	**havlu**
toilet paper	**tuvalet kağidi**
not clean	**temiz değil**
cheers!	**şerefe!**
1	**bir**
2	**iki**
3	**üç**
4	**dört**
5	**beş**
6	**alti**
7	**yedi**
8	**sekiz**
9	**dokuz**
10	**on**
11	**on bir**
12	**on iki**
13	**on üç**
20	**yirmi**
30	**otuz**
40	**kirk**
50	**elli**
60	**altmiş**
70	**yetmiş**
80	**seksen**
90	**doksan**
100	**yüz**
200	**iki yüz**
1000	**bin**
2000	**iki bin**
10,000	**on bin**
1,000,000	**milyon**

CHAPTER FIFTEEN:
WHEN THINGS GO WRONG

Turkey is a wonderful country for a holiday. The reason I start this section with such a positive and true statement is that, after you've read the next few pages, you might wonder why on earth anyone bothers to visit the place.

However, things can go wrong wherever you take your holiday. Torquay, Torremolinos or Turkey. I list the possibilities here in the certain knowledge that forewarned is forearmed, and the superstitious hope that maybe if you're ready for them, then they won't happen. If they do and you find everyone flapping around like headless chickens, you can sit back, sip your tea and make like the experienced traveller. "Of course one expects these minor hiccups in a country like this" is a winning line. "Adds to the fun of it all, I always say."

Possible minor hiccups

- *Electricity cuts*. There's often a candle and matchbox left in your room. You'll soon discover why. Pack a torch and rely on the sun to dry your hair.
- *Cold water*. This is the one that causes the most groans. It's easily explained. Water is nearly always heated by the ecologically sound solar system. When the sun goes down, no more water can be heated. As the sun goes down, everyone leaves the beach and heads home for a shower. The hot-water tanks only hold so much. You can guess the rest of the saga. Your best bet is obviously to shower earlier than the others. Or learn to love cold water.

- *Basic accommodation.* Basic in Turkey means *basic* – and probably shabby, however twee the brochures get with their descriptions. Read the notes in this book on the different accommodation standards in Turkey. If you plump for budget accommodation, remind yourself that you came on holiday to get away from things like coat-hangers, shower curtains, wall to wall carpets and G-Plan bedroom suites.
- *Noise.* The Turkish people tend to eat late and after good food and drink (which gourmets will discover is every meal) in some restaurants the clients like to sing and dance. In busy resorts, if the locals aren't singing and dancing, the holidaymakers probably are. And if the restaurants don't encourage music, the open-air bars and discos do. So if you want early nights, avoid staying in towns or near popular restaurants and bars. The Turks also like music (usually Western pop) on the beach and some of the popular beaches are wired for sound.

  And remember: the Moslem religion involves praying five times a day. Even though many Turks you meet might not follow this, the *muezzin* (or his tape-recorder) will be in the mosques at daybreak – just after the last reveller has turned in for the night – calling the faithful to prayer with the help of sturdy loudspeakers.
- *Transfer times.* Check the transfer times from airport to your resort if you're not fond of long coach rides.
- *Health.* Turkey can go to your stomach. Read the practical information notes in chapter five.
- *Theft.* This is only listed to assure you that theft is – as yet – a very rare occurrence.

Not so Turkish problems

Some things that go wrong are not so much Turkey's fault as to do with the way some travel companies conduct their business. Here's a brief run-down of what action to take when you think you are being offered a holiday different from the one you were promised by the tour operator.

Don't wait till you get home to complain. We British have a deserved reputation for suffering in silence. Instead, tell your holiday rep at once. If the problem is about your accommodation you should also tackle the hotel owner or manager if they speak English. Start with a smile. Be calm and polite but firm.

Travel with the holiday brochure and any letters, or a copy of the booking form confirming any special promises like a sea view or free windsurfing lessons. They help you argue your case.

If nothing gets done and the problem doesn't go away, you need to make detailed and dated notes of the meetings you have with the people who should be putting it all right. You might also like to ask other holidaymakers to sign a statement with their full names and addresses as witnesses to your problems.

Perhaps the room you were promised, with a sea view and close to the beach, turns out to be in an annexe half a mile away overlooking the town rubbish dump. Take photographs if they'll help strengthen your case. Pictures of the unfinished symphony of concrete that's supposed to be your peaceful garden retreat could be an asset.

If your troubles cause you to spend money you hadn't planned to, keep the receipts. This is fair advice although it's often impossible to implement in many parts of Turkey.

If nothing is done to put right a reasonable complaint, as soon as you get home, go to your travel agent if you booked through one. Show them your tan and new leather jacket, then tell them your story. Some agents will take up your case with the tour operator.

With unhelpful agents – or if you booked direct – you need to write a clear, short letter to the tour operator (the address is in the brochure and you might like to telephone for the name of the managing director and address your letter to him). In the letter include your travel dates and where you stayed and, if you have it, your booking reference number. Outline your complaint, what you did about it on holiday and what action you want the company to take. If possible have the letter typed. Date it and keep a copy. Send with it *copies* of letters, photos and statements that back up your complaint. Don't cloud the issue with unnecessary whining about unconnected issues like your bumpy flight or the noisy foreigners in the next room. If you want compensation you should say how much in the letter and add the words "without prejudice", so you're not committed to that sum.

Sadly, in most complaint cases, you must be prepared to dig in for a long fight. Prompt and generous replies from some holiday companies are as common as snowstorms in Antalya. If you're not happy with any reply you get and the company belongs to the Association of British Travel Agents (ABTA), you can ask ABTA to act as a go-between for you, using their free *conciliation* scheme. If the results of that are unsatisfactory, ABTA organises an *arbitration* scheme where an independent arbitrator makes a judgement on your case and you are obliged to settle for what he/she says. Both you and the holiday company (who has to agree to go to arbitration) pay a fee for this scheme of upwards of £23, which is usually returnable to the "winner".

Instead of the ABTA arbitration scheme you can claim compensation of (currently) up to £500 in the County Court using the small claims procedure in England and Wales. You can't do both. The County Court is also the place for complaints about non-ABTA holidays abroad. You don't need a solicitor. In fact they're discouraged and if you win you're not allowed to claim their fee.

For free legal advice and help with pursuing a serious complaint, visit your nearest Citizens' Advice Bureau or Law Centre. Their numbers are in the phone book.

If you think the holiday company described the holiday wrongly in their brochure or in a letter to you, you can report their broken promises to the Trading Standards Officer. They can take out a criminal prosecution against the company and you could be awarded damages. (By the way, if you paid for your holiday by credit card, as long as you paid the holiday company direct and not a travel agent, you can approach the credit card company for compensation.)

It's unfair but this complaining business is frustratingly hard work. It's only worth pursuing for genuine serious complaints. Contrary to pub talk, companies don't shell out handfuls of notes to so-called professional complainers to keep them quiet.

Association of British Travel Agents, 55-57 Newman Street, London W1P 4AH. Tel: 01-637 2444.

CHAPTER SIXTEEN: WHO GOES WHERE

Tour operators

No one travel agent has on its shelves brochures for every company offering holidays to Turkey. Indeed not every company sells its Turkish holidays through travel agents. Some companies are very small and you need to contact them direct to get a copy of their brochure.

The following list of companies has been compiled with the generous help of the Turkish Culture and Information Office in London.

For current information on who is selling what and for how much, you need to contact a selection of travel agents and some of these companies yourself. For a free copy of the latest up-to-date-list of holiday companies offering trips to Turkey, write to the Turkish Tourist Office at 170 Piccadilly, London W1.

If a company is a member of ABTA their membership number is quoted – see page 150 for an explanation of ABTA's arbitration scheme for complaints about their members. A company's Air Travel Organiser's Licence – ATOL – number is also quoted where applicable. Both ABTA members and ATOL holders are covered by a bond which helps repatriate stranded holidaymakers should the company financially fail.

SUMMER HOLIDAYS

A & J TOURS
146 Kingsland High Street, London E8 2NS
Tel: 01-254 8128   Telex: 269259   ABTA 88346
7 and 14 night or longer holidays in Istanbul, Izmir, Bodrum Peninsula, Olüdeniz, Kaş, and Side. Self-catering accommodation in Side only.
Fly-drive and tailor-made holidays.
Flight-only and accommodation-only facility.

ADVENTURE HOLIDAYS
10 Linden Park, Bangor, Co. Down, N. Ireland
Tel: 0247 473783
Holidays from Northern Ireland only:
Tailor-made holidays in the Bodrum area, specialising in yachting holidays.
Flight-only arrangements.

AEGEAN TURKISH HOLIDAYS
53A Salusbury Road, London NW6 6NJ
Tel: 01-372 6902   Telex: 265260   ABTA 71773   ATOL 997
7, 14 and 21 nights in Istanbul, Kuşadasi, Davutlar, Torba, Gündogdu, Akyarlar, Bodrum, Gökova, Marmaris, Turunc, Kalkan, Kaş Beldibi, Antalya, Colakli, Side, Sorgun, Alanya. A selection of self-catering villas offered with free car hire. Large selection of 2-centre holidays.
Coach tours: Trojan Horse Tour 7 nights.
Cappadocian Tour 7 nights.
Special interest: Whirling Dervishes Tour 12 nights.
Gulet cruising: 7 and 14 nights.
Fly-drive, tailor-made, flight-only available.

AEGINA CLUB
25A Hills Road, Cambridge CB2 1NW
Tel: 0223 63256   Telex: 81684 AEGINA   ATOL 0262
One or two-centre holidays of 1 and 2 week duration in Istanbul, Kuşadasi, Davutlar, Torba, Bodrum, Kaş, Kalkan, Antalya, Side, Alanya.
Fly-drive holidays of 1 to 3 weeks duration.
14 and 21 day coach tours of Western, Southern, Central and Eastern Turkey.
Tailor-made and flight-only arrangements.
Coastal cruises.

ALLEGRO HOLIDAYS
15A Church Street, Reigate, Surrey RH2 0AA
Tel: 0737 221323   Telex: 919114 ALEGRO G
ABTA 12173   ATOL 1835
7 and 14 day holidays in Antalya, Alanya, Side.
Tailor-made and 2-centre-request.
Fly-drive, flight-only arrangements.

AQUARIUS TRAVEL
Western House, 9 Glandovey Terrace, Aberdovey, Gwynedd
LL35 0EB
Tel: 0654 72646   Telex: 35746 AQRSTL G
7, 14 and 21 nights at new studio apartments in beachfront villa, at Bitez, near Bodrum.
Fly-drive, tailor-made and accommodation-only.

AQUASPORT TOURS LTD.
181 Edward Street, Brighton BN2 2JB
Tel: 0273 685824 or 0273 685187
7, 14, 21 and 28 day FLY-DRIVE (Motor caravans, estate cars with camping pack, motor boats with camping pack), camping, village rooms at: Antalya, Bodrum, Fethiye, Göcek, Izmir, Marmaris.
14, 21, 28 day watersports holidays (diving, sailboarding, waterskiing) at Göcek.
1 to 3 week gulet cruising from Bodrum, Marmaris and Göcek.

BALKAN TOURS LTD.
10 Lombard Street, Belfast BT1 1RB
Tel: 0232-246795 or 325902   Telex: 747988
ABTA 1510X   ATOL 1171
May-October, 7/14 nights in Ayvalik, Çeşme, Kuşadasi. 7 day coach tour.
Bulgaria-Turkey 2-centre 14 days.
Fly-drive, tailor-made, flight-only, accommodation-only.

BEACH VILLAS (HOLIDAYS) LTD.
8 Market Passage, Cambridge CB2 3QR
Tel: 0223 311113   Telex: 817428 BCHVLA
ABTA 1415X   ATOL 381B
2 week beachside villa and apartment holidays in Bodrum and Gümüslük.
Fly-drive holidays.

BEST YACHTING AND TOURISM
Kargi Marine, Hillier House, 509 Upper Richmond Road, London SW14 7EE
Tel: 01-873 3227   Telex: 9413819 HILHOU G
Self-catering villas, apartments, traditional cottages and houses available for 7-28 days, on the Bodrum Peninsula, the Gulfs of Fethiye and Finike and in a mountain village in the South, and in Ünye and Trabzon on the Black Sea. Also small pensions.
7-14 day sail/cruise/stay, 7-21 day 2-centre combining Istanbul or Bursa with a resort or sailing holiday.
Fly-drive, tailor-made and accommodation booking service.

THE BLUE EYE TOUR COMPANY
3 Albion Hill, Loughton, Essex IG10 4RA
Tel: 01-508 1930
2 week or longer apartment holidays in Datça.
Special interest: 1 week in Istanbul for retired people, throughout the year.

BLUESPOT TRAVEL LTD.
28 Maddox Street, London W1R 9PF
Tel: 01-408 0094 or 01-409 3034   Telex: 297547 BLUSPT G
ATOL 2113
7 and 14 nights and flexible arrangements in Kuşadasi, Bodrum, Marmaris, Turunc, Ölü Deniz, Kalkan, Kaş, Kemer, Antalya, Side, Izmir, Çeşme and Istanbul. (2-centre and multi-centre holidays can be arranged).
14 day EASTERN TURKEY Coach Tour.
Fly-drive, tailor-made, flight-only, accommodation-only arrangements.

BOSPHORUS HOLIDAYS
Silver House, 31-35 Beak Street, London W1R 3LD
Tel: 01-437 7316   Telex: 296398 BOSPOR
3 nights to 3 months or longer, in Istanbul, Izmir, Çeşme, Kuşadasi, Bodrum, Marmaris, Antalya, Side, Alanya and Mersin.
Special interest tours of 3 nights to 3 months can be arranged for individuals and groups.
Fly-drive, tailor-made and flight-only arrangements.

CARRINGTON CLASSICS
7 Elms Avenue, Eastbourne, Sussex
Tel: 0323 647302   ATOL 31827
14 nights holiday in Dalyan.
Coach tours to Marmaris and Fethiye one day at each.
River trips to Caunus and Köycegiz.

CELEBRITY HOLIDAYS AND TRAVEL
18 Frith Street, London W1V 5TS
Tel: 01-439 1961 or 01-734 4386   Telex: 269304
ABTA 18659   ATOL 1469
3, 5, 7 and 14 day holidays in Istanbul. 14 day holidays in Kuşadasi, Bodrum, Marmaris, Ölü Deniz, Kalkan, Antalya, Side. Two-centre holidays.
Fly-drive, tailor-made, flight-only arrangements.

CLUB MEDITERRANEE
106/110 Brompton Road, London SW3 1JJ
Tel: 01-226 1066 or 01-581 4769   ABTA 19685   ATOL 1020
1 week or more at Club Med's holiday villages in Foça, Kuşadasi, Kemer, Palmiye. Prices include all sports facilities and tuition.

CLUB SPORTIF
(Part of Grosvenor Hall Leisure)
Grosvenor Hall, Bolnore Road, Haywards Heath, Sussex RH16 4BX
Tel: 0444 441300   Telex: 877156   ABTA 54369   ATOL 1068
1 or 2 week sporting holidays at Club Alba, Antalya (tennis, windsurfing, sailing, diving, riding, waterskiing, cycling, health and fitness, archery, etc.).
Tailor-made holidays available.

CLUB TURKEY
113 Upper Richmond Road, Putney, London SW15 2TL
Tel: 01-785 6389   Telex: 926631 CLUBTY G   ATOL 754
7/14/21 nights in Istanbul, Antalya, Side, Alanya, Kemer, Kaş, Kalkan.
Tailor-made holidays.

CONTIKI HOLIDAYS
Wells House, 15 Elmfield Road, Bromley BR1 1LS
Tel: 01-290 6777   ABTA 20305   ATOL 1274
7 and 14 nights in Datça at a resort exclusive to 18-35 year olds. Free water-sports, private beach.
7 night mini-bus tour of Central Turkey, round trip from Datça.
Tailor-made holidays.

COSMOSAIR PLC
Tourama House, 17 Homesdale Road, Bromley BR2 9LX
Tel: 01-464 3444   Telex: 896458   ABTA 23318   ATOL 2275
7 and 14 nights in Kuşadasi, Bodrum, Marmaris and Alanya.
Coach tours: Highlights of Western Turkey and Istanbul.
Highlights of Central Turkey, Istanbul.
Flight-only arrangements.

CRUSADER CRUISING
14 Lissel Road, Simpson, Milton Keynes MK6 3AX
Tel: 0908 670346   Telex: 825264 SILBUS
1/2/3 week self-catering, hotel and camping holidays in Bodrum and the surrounding area.
Tailor-made holidays: 1/2/3 week Istanbul, Izmir.
Fly-drive, flight-only and accommodation-only can be arranged.

C.T.A. HOLIDAYS LTD.
28 Cockspur Street, London SW1Y 5BN
Tel: 01-930 4853   Telex: 885614   ABTA 19261   ATOL 1000B
Up to 4 weeks in Istanbul, or as part of a two-centre Istanbul-North Cyprus holiday throughout the year.
Fly-drive, tailor-made, flight-only, accommodation-only arrangements.

CYGNUS WILDLIFE HOLIDAYS LTD.
96 Fore Street, Kingsbridge, Devon TQ7 1PY
Tel: 0548 6178   Telex: 45772 TACOMM G
15 day Birdwatching holidays, led by experienced ornithological leader.

DALYAN HOLIDAYS (Bon Voyage Ltd.)
1 Buckingham Way, Frimley, Camberley, Surrey
Tel: 0276 65460
1 to 4 week holidays in Dalyan. Good choice of local hotels. An area of wildlife and archaeological interest. Holidays arranged all year round.
Tailor-made holidays and accommodation-only can be arranged.
Gulet cruising from Göcek for any duration.

DELTASUN HOLIDAYS
58 Paddington Street, London W1M 3RR
Tel: 01-487 4503 or 01-935 9535   Telex: 265685 DSUN G
ATOL 2167
1, 2 and 3 week holidays in Istanbul, Kuşadasi, Bodrum, Marmaris, Datça, Fethiye, Ölü Deniz, Kalkan, Kaş, Antalya, Side, Alanya.
Coach tours: Western Anatolia (1 week)
            Central Anatolia (1 week)
            Anatolian Highlights (2 weeks)
Fly-drive, tailor-made, flight-only and accommodation-only arrangements.

E.C. BUREAU
Dunstown, Mintlaw AB4 7UJ, Scotland
Tel: 077982 249
Weekly or monthly villa rentals throughout the year at Kabakum near Dikili on the Aegean Coast. Car hire can be arranged.

ENTERPRISE – REDWING HOLIDAYS
Groundstar House, London Road, Crawley, West Sussex RH10 2TB
Tel: 0293 517866 (Reserv.) or 0293 560777 (Admin.)   Telex: 878791
ABTA 95301   ATOL 2366
7 and 14 night hotel and apartment holidays in Kuşadasi, Altinkum, Gümbet (Bodrum), Marmaris, Içmeler, Kemer and Side.
Flight-only arrangements.

EURO AMERICAN TRAVEL
18 Hertford Street, Coventry CV1 1LF
Tel: 0203 630709   Telex: MBX 203630703   ABTA 94262
7 and 14 day holidays in Istanbul, Bursa, Konya and other places which are of interest to Moslem visitors.
Flight and accommodation service.

EXODUS EXPEDITIONS
All Saints Passage, 100 Wandsworth High Street, London
SW18 4LE
Tel: 01-870 0151   Telex: 8951700   ATOL 355B
Various adventure tours of 15, 16 and 24 days' duration, using a combination of camping and pansiyon accommodation.
Walking holidays of 15 and 23 days' duration, camping and village accommodation.
15 day 'Winter in Turkey' tour.

EXPLORE WORLDWIDE LTD.
7 High Street, Aldershot, Hants GU11 1BH
Tel: 0252 319448   Telex: 858954 EXPLOR G
A variety of adventure trips of 16 and 23 days' duration, mostly small hotel and guesthouse accommodation.
16 day Seatrek from Antalya to Marmaris.
16 day winter walking tour.

FALCON HOLIDAYS
33 Notting Hill Gate, London W11 3JQ
Tel: 01-221 6298   Telex: 922889   ABTA 68342   ATOL 1337
1 and 2 week holidays in Kuşadasi, Altinkum, Golköy, Gündogan Bodrum, Gümbet, Türlbükü, Marmaris, Içmeler, Kemer, Beldibi and Side.
Two-centre Turkey/Greece.
1 week 'Classical' coach tour.
1 week gulet cruises.
Flight-only arrangements.

FALCON SAILING
33 Notting Hill Gate, London W11 3JQ
Tel: 01-727 0232   Telex: 922889 (Attn. SAILING)
ABTA 68342   ATOL 1337
1 and 2 week windsurfing holidays in Yalıkavak, and dinghy sailing/windsurfing holidays in Bitez, both with Royal Yachting Association tuition.
Tailor-made windsurfing/dinghy sailing/yachting packages.

FATOSH TRAVEL
54 Green Lanes, Palmers Green N13
Tel: 01-888 0706 (6 lines)   Telex: 918494
7/14/21 nights in Kuşadası, Gümüldür, Bodrum, Marmaris, Fethiye, Side.
Special breaks in Istanbul and Izmir.
Tailor-made holidays, fly-drive, flight-only, accommodation-only arrangements.

FIRST RESORT HOLIDAYS
London House, Old Court Place, 26-40 Kensington High Street, London W8 4PF
Tel: 01-938 3492   Telex: 94017418 FRES G
ABTA 29032   ATOL 2097
7 and 14 night holidays in Istanbul.
7, 14, 21 and 28 nights in Marmaris, Ölü Deniz and Side, in hotels, apartments and pansiyons.
Waterskiing tuition for beginners at Ölü Deniz.
Tailor-made holidays, flight-only, accommodation-only arrangements.
7 and 14 night fully crewed gulet cruises from Fethiye.

GALAXY HOLIDAYS
Pillar and Lucy House, Merchants Road, Gloucester GL1 5RG
Tel: 0452 308798
June and September 1989. 1 week tours including Istanbul, Bursa, Çanakkale, Izmir (visiting Pergamon, Ephesus and Troy).

GOLDEN HORN TRAVEL
Golden House, 29 Great Pulteney Street, London W1R 3DD
Tel: 01-434 1962 (Reserv.) or 01-439 3029 (Admin.)
Telex: 298287 GLDTR G   ABTA 31193   ATOL 1751
1 and 2 week holiday in Istanbul, Kuşadası, Bodrum, Marmaris, Kemer, Antalya, Side and Alanya.
Two-Centre: Istanbul with any of the above. Kuşadası with Bodrum.
Coach tours: 14 day Cappadocia tours, historic South West tours, classical tours.
Self-catering holidays, tailor-made holidays.
Fly-drive, flight-only, accommodation-only arrangements.

HAMILTON TRAVEL LTD.
3 Heddon Street, London W1R 7LE
Tel: 01-439 3199   Telex: 299176   ABTA 79281   ATOL 1489
Year round holidays in Istanbul of 2 nights to 1 month duration.
Fly-drive, tailor-made holidays, flight-only arrangements.

HANN OVERLAND (HIGHCREST TRAVEL LTD.)
Overland Tours
2nd Floor 268-270 Vauxhall Bridge Road, London SW1V 1EJ
Tel: 01-834 7337   Telex: 914846 HANN OV G
Coach tours: 22 days Eastern Turkey and Black Sea. 16 days Göreme and South Coast.
Göreme walking tour – 7-10 days.
Short treks – Eastern Turkey.
Flight-only arrangements.

HCI CLUB HOLIDAYS
4 Broadway, Edgbaston Five Ways, Birmingham B15 1BB
Tel: 021-643 2727   Telex: 335641   ABTA 35391   ATOL 169
7 and 14 nights at Club Santana, Alanya, with free sports and entertainment.
Flight-only arrangements.

HIGHWAY HOLIDAYS
63 Grays Inn Road, London WC1X 8TL
Tel: 01-405 1368   Telex: 8952517   ATOL 89
Coach Tours: 'In the Steps of St. Paul' plus Istanbul, Izmir, Pamukkale, etc. 12 days.
'The Seven Churches and Byzantium' plus Istanbul, Adana, Tarsus, Göreme Valley, Konya, etc. 13 days.
Tailor-made holidays.

HOLIDAYRAMA
23/25 Procter Street, London WC1V 6NS
Tel: 01-831 8440 or 01-405 4355   Telex: 267224 BEEHIV
ABTA 83380   ATOL 2135
7 and 14 night holidays in Istanbul, Kuşadası, Güzelçamlı, Altinkum, Bodrum, Ortakent, Marmaris, Çalis, Ölü Deniz, Alanya.
Two-centre: Istanbul/Resort.
Coach tours: 7 days – from Izmir Cappadocia – from Ismir Classical – from Dalaman Wonders of Turkey.
Fly-drive holidays; flight-only arrangements.
3, 7, 14 day cruises departing from Bodrum, Marmaris, Fethiye, Antalya.

HORIZON HOLIDAYS LTD.
4 Broadway, Edgbaston Five Ways, Birmingham B15 1BB
Tel: 021-643 2727   Telex: 335641 HORIZON G
ABTA 35391   ATOL 169
7 and 14 night holidays in Alanya, Side, Marmaris, Bodrum, Hotels and apartments.
Flight-only arrangements.

DAVID HOUSELEY (Travel Consultants)
152 Colneis Road, Felixstowe, Suffolk IP11 9LQ
Tel: 0394 283525
15 day 'Seven Churches of Asia' coach tour.
Special arrangements for Church groups.

ILIOS ISLAND HOLIDAYS
18 Market Square, Horsham, W. Sussex RH12 1EU
Tel: 0403 59788   Telex: 878168 ILIOS G
ABTA 76635   ATOL 1452
1-2 week self-catering holidays in select villas and apartments in Akyaka.
Fly-drive and tailor-made holidays, flight-only arrangements.

INTASUN HOLIDAYS
Intasun House, Cromwell Avenue, Bromley, Kent BR2 9AQ
Tel: 01-290 0511 or 01-290 1900 (Res.)   Telex: 896089
ABTA 3691X   ATOL 1960
Summer 1989 Brochure.
7, 10, 11 and 14 days in Kuşadası, Altınkum, Bodrum/Gümbet, Bitez, Torba, Marmaris, Datça and Fethiye.
7 and 14 days in Alanya and Side.
A wide choice of quality accommodation.

Summer 1989 – Turkey – Plain and Simple Brochure: 7, 10, 11, 14, 21 days in Ayvalik, Foça, Çeşme, Kuşadası, Altınkum, Torba, Bodrum/Gümbet, Bitez, Ortakent, Akyarlar, Turgutreis, Marmaris/ Içmeler, Datça, Fethiye, Patara, Kaş.
7, 14, 21 days in Alanya and Side.
Accommodation in pansiyons, motels, hotels and apartments. A wide range of two-centre holidays.
Coach tours.
Fly-drive holidays; flight-only arrangements.

INTER-CHURCH TRAVEL LTD.
The Saga Building, Middelburg Square, Folkestone, Kent
CT20 1AZ
Tel: 0303 47535   Telex: 966331   ABTA: 36869   ATOL: 308B
Coach Tours:
'The Journey of St. Paul' 11 nights Turkey/Cyprus.
'In the Steps of St. Paul' 12 nights Turkey/Greece.
'Black Sea Coast and Eastern Turkey' 13 nights.
'Istanbul, Cappadocia, Antakya' 10 nights.
Tailor-made holidays.

INTRA TRAVEL LTD.
121-122 Tottenham Court Road, London W1P 9NH
Tel: 01-383 7701   Telex: 928652 INTRA G   ATOL: 2392
7 and 14 nights in Istanbul, Şile, Kuşadasi, Bodrum, Marmaris, Fethiye, Kalkan, Kaş, Kemer, Antalya, Side, Alanya. Also 2-centre holidays.
Coach tours: Biblical, Archaeological, Ottoman.
Conference/incentives.
School trips.
Fly-drive and tailor-made holiday, flight-only and accommodation-only arrangements.

JENNY MAY HOLIDAYS
35 St. John's Hill, London SW11 1TT
Tel: 01-228 0321   Telex: 915320 JMHOLS G
1, 2, 3 week villa holidays (some luxury with pools) in Bodrum, Bodrum Peninsula and Marmaris, from March to November.
1, 2, 3 week crewed gulet cruises.
Fly-drive, tailor-made, flight-only, accommodation-only.

LANCASTER HOLIDAYS
26 Elmfield Road, Bromley, Kent BR1 1LR
Tel: 01-697 8181   Telex: 8953010 LANAIR G
ABTA 3691X   ATOL 1960
Travel Turkey – North and South (two brochures) offering 7, 14, 21 night holidays in Erdek, Ayvalık, Foça, Ceşme, Kuşadasi, Altınkum, Bodrum, Gümbet, Ortakent, Turgutreis, Akyarlar, Güvercinlik, Marmaris, Içmeler, Gökova, Turunc, Datça, Fethiye, Çalış, Patara, Kalkan, Kaş, Antalya, Side, Alanya.
3 and 4 night Istanbul City Breaks.
Two-centre holidays. Coach and Stay holidays. 7 night Coach Tours; Jeep Tours from Fethiye.

LOGOTOUR LTD.
189 Regent Street, London W1R 7WE
Tel: 01-437 0535 or 0587   Telex: 265114 LOGOTR
ABTA: 42817   ATOL: 2280
7 and 14 night holidays in Istanbul, on the Aegean and Mediterranean Coasts, throughout the year.
Fly-drive, tailor-made holidays.
Flight-only, accommodation-only service.

MARK WARNER
20 Kensington Church Street, London W8 4EP
Tel: 01-938 1851   Telex: 24304 SKIMWT   ABTA 20358
1 and 2 week holidays in Club hotels in the Bodrum area, with free watersports tuition.

METAK HOLIDAYS
69/70 Welbeck Street, London W1M 7HA
Tel: 01-935 6961   Telex: 263188   ABTA 43858   ATOL 1116
3, 4, 5, 7, 10 and 14 day holidays in Istanbul, Izmir and Antalya.
7 and 14 days in Kuşadası, Bodrum, Kemer, Side, Alanya.
Two and three-centre holidays, fly-drive and tailor-made holidays.
10 and 14 day coach tours which can be combined with a beach holiday.
7 day yacht cruises from Bodrum, and combinations of cruise and stay holidays.
Flight-only and accommodation-only service.

MOSAIC HOLIDAYS
Tri-Sun House, Station Approach, Broadway, Yaxley, Peterborough PE7 3EE
Tel: 0733 244994   Telex: 32134 NNISAS G
ABTA 99567   ATOL 2470
7 and 14 day holidays in Istanbul, Çeşme, Kuşadası, Kemer, Beldibi, Side and Alanya.
Two-centre: Istanbul/North Cyprus.
Fly-drive and flight-only arrangements.
Coach tours: 15 days Western Turkey.

MOSAIC SELECT
73 South Audley Street, London W1Y 5FF
Tel: 01-493 3380   Telex: 918090 NNISAS G   ABTA 99567
10 and 14 night coach tours of Eastern Turkey, Black Sea Coast, Cappadocia, Turkey/North Cyprus.
Tailor-made holidays.

ORIENTOURS (LONDON) LTD.
Kent House, 87 Regent Street, London W1R 8LS
Tel: 01-434 1551   Telex: 21337   ABTA 46485   ATOL 781B
Coach Tours:
'Seven Churches of Asia' including Istanbul – 11 days.
Cappadocia and Antalya – 12 days.
Eastern Turkey – 12/14 days.
Fly-drive and tailor-made holidays, flight-only and accommodation-only arrangements.

OVERSEAS CAMPING TOURS LTD.
181 Edward Street, Brighton BN2 2JB
Tel: 0273 685824 or 0273 685187
7, 14, 21 and 28 day fly-drive (motor caravans, estate cars with camping pack, motor boats with camping pack), camping and village room holidays, in Antalya, Fethiye, Göcek, Marmaris, Bodrum, Izmir.
Watersports holidays (diving, sailboarding, waterskiing) in Göcek.
Tailor-made holidays.

PAGE & MOY LTD.
136-140 London Road, Leicester LE2 1EN
Tel: 0533 542000   Telex: 34583   ABTA 47026   ATOL 133
10 night 'Ancient Turkey' tour.

THE PERSONAL TRAVEL COMPANY
16A Terrapin Road, London SW17 8QN
Tel: 01-673 8390
1 week or longer holidays in Bodrum, Gölköy, Akyarlar, in traditional villas, tailor-made for the individual, family or group.
Winter breaks in Bodrum (1 week or longer).
Fly-drive and flight-only available.

PROSPECT MUSIC AND ART LTD.
10 Barley Mew Passage, Chiswick, London W4 4PH
Tel: 01-995 2163 or 01-995 2151   Telex: 918705   ATOL 2147
Art/Archaeological Tours: 5 days – Istanbul; 8 days – Istanbul, Bursa, Edirne; 13 days – South West Coast, from Izmir to Antalya; 16 days – Central and Eastern Turkey.
4 night Winter Breaks in Istanbul.

RAINBOW SAILING
Cardinal House, Church Row, Wernffrwd, Swansea SA4 3TT
Tel: 0792 467813   Telex: 94015991 RAIN G
Villa accommodation or villa/sail combination holidays in the Marmaris area. Any duration.
Tailor-made holidays.
Accommodation-only.

RAMBLERS HOLIDAYS LTD.
Box 43, Welwyn Garden City, Herts AL8 6PQ
Tel: 0707 331133   Telex: 24642 RTOUR G
ABTA 50940   ATOL 990
Highlights of Eastern Turkey, 2 week multi-centre tour.
Kuşadası and Fethiye, 2 week sightseeing/walking tour.
Trabzon and Erzurum, 2 week walking tour.
Istanbul – 1 week sightseeing/easy walking tour throughout the year.
Accommodation booking.

REGENT HOLIDAYS (UK) LTD.
Regent House, 31A High Street, Shanklin, Isle of Wight PO37 6JW
Tel: 0983 864212 or 0983 864225   Telex: 86197
ABTA 51587   ATOL 856
Holidays in Istanbul, Kilyos, Ankara, Erdek, Izmir, Bodrum, Gümbet, Turgutreis, Beldibi, Antalya, Side.
Horse riding holidays, gulet cruises ex Bodrum and Marmaris.
Coach tours: 7 and 12 nights.
Fly-drive, tailor-made holidays, flight-only and accommodation-only arrangements.

SAMSON TRAVEL LTD.
127 Kingsland High Street, London E8 2PB
Tel: 01-240 2687 or 01-240 5111   Telex: 927666 SAMSON G
ABTA 90755
1 to 4 week holidays in Istanbul.
1 to 3 week self-catering and hotel holidays in Ören, Kuşadası, Bodrum, Yalıkavak, Datça, Side and Alanya.
1 and 2 week hunting holidays.
1 and 2 week yacht cruises from Bodrum and Marmaris.
Car-hire, fly-drive, flight-only, accommodation-only arrangements.

SAVILE TRAVEL AND TOURS
32 Maddox Street, London W1
Tel: 01-499 5101   Telex: 269529   ATOL 2042
7, 10 and 14 day holidays in Istanbul (Ottoman Palaces, Mansions and Pensions), Bursa, Kuşadası, Bodrum, Türkbükü, Kalkan, Antalya.
Special fully guided tour to the war graves of Gallipoli and to Troy, including 3 nights in Istanbul.
Cappadocia tour, combined with Ankara and Istanbul, using sleeper trains as part of the transport.
Fly-drive and tailor-made holidays, flight-only, accommodation-only arrangements.

SCHOOL TRAVEL SERVICE
24 Culloden Road, Enfield, Middlesex EN2 8QD
Tel: 01-363 8202   Telex: 267444   ABTA 54265   ATOL 103
9 day school party tour by air at Easter.
Istanbul.
Istanbul-Bursa-Izmir.

SERENISSIMA TRAVEL
21 Dorset Square, London NW1 6QG
Tel: 01-730 9841 or 723 6556   Telex: 914032 or 28441
ABTA 54693   ATOL 883B
4 days in Istanbul.
19 days in Eastern Turkey (Istanbul, Trabzon, Erzurum, Sarıkamış, Dogubeyazıt, Van).
9 days in Istanbul, Iznik, Bursa, Edirne.

SHERPA EXPEDITIONS
131A Heston Road, Hounslow TW5 0RD
Tel: 01-577 2717   Telex: 892512   ATOL 1185B
16 day mountain walking/trekking holidays – Eastern and Southern Turkey.

SILVERSAND HOLIDAYS LTD.
17B Riding House Street, London W1P 7PB
Tel: 01-637 8728   Telex: 262598 SILVER G
7, 14 and 21 night holidays in Istanbul, Kuşadası, Bodrum, Marmaris, Kemer, Antalya, Side, Alanya.
Two-Centre holidays.
7 and 14 day Western and Central Coach Tours.
Fly-drive and tailor-made holidays, flight-only and accommodation arrangements.

SIMPLY TURKEY
486 Chiswick High Road, London W4 5TT
Tel: 01-747 1011   Telex: 8955503 SIMPLY G   ATOL 2302
1, 2 or 3 week holidays Akyarlar, Ortakent, Gümüşlük, Akyaka, Ölü Deniz. Mainly self-catering but also some pansiyon accommodation.
1, 2 or 3 week special interest (wild flowers, painting, archaeological, wild boar hunting, scuba diving) holidays which can be combined with a Blue Cruise. 1/2/3 week gulet cruises.
Fly-drive and tailor-made holidays, flight-only.

SMALL WORLD SUN
2 Mount Sion, Tunbridge Wells, Kent TN1 1UE
Tel: 0892 511733   Telex: 94070357 SSUN
ABTA 9421X   ATOL 2318
7 and 14 night House Parties at Güllük and Torba which can be combined with gulet cruising.
14 night Turkey/Greece two-centre House Party (Torba and Kalymnos).
7 day gulet cruises (can be combined with House Party holidays – 2 weeks).

SOVEREIGN HOLIDAYS – REDWING HOLIDAYS
Groundstar House, London Road, Crawley RH10 2TB
Tel: 0293 560777   Telex: 878847 REDPRO G
ABTA 95301   ATOL 2366
7 or 14 night holidays in Kuşadası, Bodrum, Antalya and Side.

STALLARD HOLIDAYS
29 Stoke Newington Road, London N16 8BL
Tel: 01-254 6444   Telex: 265010 STAG G   ABTA 56472
1-14 night holidays in Istanbul. Year round Short Break programmes – very flexible, will tailor itineraries to clients' needs.
Fly-drive holidays.

STEEPWEST HOLIDAYS LTD.
449 Oxford Street, London W1R 1DA
Tel: 01-629 2879   Telex: 297979   ABTA 55395   ATOL 1898
7 and 14 night holidays in Istanbul, Şile, Izmir, Kuşadası, Bodrum, Marmaris, Datça, Göcek, Fethiye, Patara, Kalkan, Kaş, Antalya, Side and Alanya. Two-centre holidays. Diving holidays. 7 night Central Turkey, 14 night Eastern Turkey coach tours.
7 and 14 night Blue Cruise.
Fly-drive and tailor-made holidays, flight-only, accommodation-only arrangements.

SUNFARE HOLIDAYS
35 Virginia Street, Glasgow G1 3TX
Tel: 041-552 5382 or 041-552 2711   Telex: 779480
ABTA 1337   ATOL 230
1, 2 and 3 week self-catering and bed and breakfast holidays, direct from Glasgow, in Marmaris and Kuşadası.
Flight-only arrangements.

SUNMED HOLIDAYS – REDWING HOLIDAYS
Groundstar House, London Road, Crawley, West Sussex
Tel: 0293 560777   Telex: 878791   ABTA 95301   ATOL 2366
1, 2 and 3 week holidays in Istanbul, Şile, Kilyos, Ören, Ayvalık, Kuşadası, Altınkum, Bodrum, Gümbet, Turgutreis, Ortakent, Marmaris, Icmeler, Ölü Deniz, Patara, Cavus, Kemer, Side.
1 week Walking Holidays.
1, 2 or 3 week gulet cruising from Bodrum, Marmaris and Kemer, can be combined with a resort holiday.
Tailor-made holidays, car hire, flight-only, accommodation-only.

SUNQUEST HOLIDAYS LTD.
Aldine House, Aldine Place, 141/142 Uxbridge Road, London W12
Tel: 01-749 9933 (Res.) or 01-749 9911 (Admin.)   Telex: 22319
ABTA 57352   ATOL 754
1 week or longer in Istanbul and Istanbul resorts, Kuşadası, Bodrum, Fethiye, Çalış, Kalkan, Antalya, Side, Alanya.
2 week Two-centre holidays, fly-drive holidays, tailor-made holidays, flight-only, accommodation-only.
14 night coach tours: Istanbul/Alanya/Cappadocia; Alanya/Cappadocia; Kuşadası/Cappadocia.

SWAN HELLENIC ART TREASURES TOURS
77 New Oxford Street, London WC1A 1PP
Tel: 01-831 1234 (Admin.) or 01-831 1616 (Reserv.)   Telex: 885551
ABTA 27427   ATOL 0307
19 day Art Treasures Tour of Anatolia: (Central Turkey, Mediterranean, Aegean and Istanbul).
17 day Art Treasures Tour of Istanbul, Western and Southern Turkey.
20 day Arts Treasures Tour of Eastern Turkey. Tours accompanied by tour manager and guest lecturer.

THOMAS COOK FARAWAY HOLIDAYS
P.O. Box 36, Thorpe Wood, Peterborough PE9 3SN
Tel: 0733 503203   ABTA 20606   ATOL 265
Russia and Beyond Brochure: 10 days out of a 20 day Tour spent in Turkey, visiting Istanbul, Ankara, Kayseri, Erzurum.

THOMSON HOLIDAYS
Greater London House, Hampstead Road, London NW1 7SD
Tel: 01-387 9321   Telex: 261123   ABTA 58213   ATOL 152
7 and 14 night holidays from May to October, in Bodrum, Gümbet, Bitez, Gümüslük, Fethiye, Caliş Beach, Ölü Deniz, Kalkan, Kaş, Kemer, Beldibi, Side, Alanya.
3 and 4 night breaks in Istanbul from March to October.
7 night coach tour of Western Turkey, plus option of 7 nights' stay in Kemer or Alanya.
7 night gulet cruising.
Fly-drive holidays, flight-only service.

TIMSWAY HOLIDAYS
Nightingales Corner, Little Chalfont, Bucks HP7 9QS
Tel: 02404 5541   Telex: 837179   ABTA 6808X   ATOL 1107
7, 14 and 21 night holidays in Kuşadası, Güzelçamlı, Gümüslük, Akyarlar and Side. 7 nights 'South Anatolia', 'Istanbul', 'Wooden Horse and Minarets' coach tours.
Fly-drive holidays, flight-only arrangements.
7 night 'Gulf of Gökova' and 'Gulf of Datça' Cruises.

TJAEREBORG LTD.
194 Campden Hill Road, London W8 7TH
Tel: 01-727 2680   Telex: 298910   ATOL 1071
7, 14, 21 and 28 night hotel holidays in Bodrum and Marmaris.
Fly-drive holidays, flight-only and accommodation-only service.

TOPAZ TRAVEL
7 Hartismere Road, London SW6 7TS
Tel: 01-381 5189 (3 lines)   Telex: 927526 TOPAZ G
ATOL Agents for 754B
7 and 14 night 'stay-put' and 4/10 night Two-centre holidays (Three-centre also available), in Istanbul Kuşadası, Bodrum, Bitez Türkbükü, Torba, Kalkan, Kaş, Kekova, Silifke, Kizkalesi.
Educational, Flora and Fauna, Archaeological tours and tailor-made itineraries organised with/without lecturers.
7 and 14 night coach tours, with 7 night resort or Blue Cruise option.
7 and 14 night Blue Cruises.
Fly-drive; tailor-made holidays, flight-only and accommodation-only service.

TOP DECK TRAVEL
131/133 Earls Court Road, London SW5 9RH
Tel: 01-244 8641   Telex: 8955339   ABTA 59767   ATOL 2057
Overland tours, spending between 3 and 17 days in Turkey and visiting Istanbul, Gallipoli, Troy, Bursa, Ephesus, Pamukkale, Fethiye, Manavgat, Silifke, Göreme, Erzurum, Reyhanlı and Dogubeyazit.

TOPSUN HOLIDAY AND TRAVEL
Groat House, Collingwood Street, Newcastle-upon-Tyne NE1 1XU
Tel: 091-222 1362   Telex: 934999 TXLINK G   Ref. MBX066133098
Tailor-made holidays; flight-only and accommodation-only arrangements.

TOURKEY TRAVEL
49 Pembridge Road, London W11 3HG
Tel: 01-243 0383   Telex: 8953686   ATOL Agent for 2167
1 or 2 weeks self-catering apartment and villa and hotel holidays in Istanbul, Kuşadası, Didim, Bodrum, Marmaris, Fethiye, Kalkan, Kemer, Antalya, Side and Alanya.
Special interest: Birdwatching, Istanbul Festival, Hunting tours.
Blue Cruises and coach tours.
Fly-drive and tailor-made holidays, flight-only and accommodation-only service.

TRANSGLOBAL LTD
64 Kenway Road, London SW5 0RD
Tel: 01-244 8571   Telex: 938358 GLOBAL
8 fully-escorted 15/22 day tours for active travellers and young people. Hotel and camping options available: 'Aegean Sailtrek', 'Turkey Land and Sea', 'Turkey Adventurer', 'Turkey Discoverer', 'Turkey Explorer', 'Black Sea and Beyond'.
4/5 day gulet cruising from Bodrum and Datça.
Tailor-made itineraries.

THE TRAVEL ALTERNATIVE LTD.
27 Park End Street, Oxford, OX1 4HU
Tel: 0865 791636   Telex: 83201 BIZCOM Attn: T/A
Three 16 to 19 day tours for small groups, with hotel accommodation: 'Cappadocian Experience', 'Eastern Turkey Wildlife Adventure', 'Nomadic Village Exploration'.
Flight-only arrangements.

THE TRAVEL CLUB OF UPMINSTER
54 Station Road, Upminster, Essex RM14 2TT
Tel: 04022 25000   Telex: 897124 TRAVEL G
ABTA 59165   ATOL 172
1 and 2 week hotel and apartment holidays in Side.

TRAVELSCENE LTD.
11/15 St. Ann's Road, Harrow HA1 1AS
Tel: 01-427 4445   Telex: 265647   ABTA 5956X   ATOL 034
Year round 3 and 7 night holidays in Istanbul.

TRESELDA LTD.
7 Granville House, 49 The Mall, Faversham, Kent
Tel: 0795 539603 or 0795 533763   Telex: 96446 SOLID G
Istanbul (3-28 days) and two-centre with any resort.
7 to 28 day holidays in Amasra, Inebolu, Bulancak (Black Sea), Princes Islands, (Sea of Marmara), Erdek, Bursa, Ayvalık, Datça (Aegean), and Bogsak, Tasucu, Kızkalesi, Arsuz (Eastern Mediterranean).
Trekking Holidays (Black Sea Coast and Mountains). Rover Holidays (all areas).
Tailor-made, fly-drive holidays. flight-only and accommodation-only arrangements.
15 day cruise from Istanbul to Alanya.

TURKEY TODAY
44 High Street, Avening, Tetbury, Glos. GL8 8NF
Tel: 0453 834028
7, 14, 21 and 28 day one and two centre holidays in hotels, pansiyons or self-catering, at Alanya, Anamur and Tasucu, which can be combined with North Cyprus.
Fly-drive, tailor-made, flight-only, accommodation only arrangements.

TURKISH CONNECTIONS
Golden House, 29 Gt. Pulteney Street, London W1R 3DD
Tel: 01-439 7406 (Reserv.) or 01-439 3020 (Admin.)
Telex: 298287 GLD TR G ABTA 31193 ATOL 1751
3-28 day holidays in Istanbul. 1-4 week holidays in Kuşadası, Bodrum, Marmaris, Kaş, Kemer, Antalya, Side, Alanya. Also, two-centre holidays. Blue Cruises (4 to 7 days).
Student travel: Hostels, cheap pansiyons (7 to 30 days).
Coach tours, tailor-made holidays, self-catering holidays. flight-only, accommodation-only service.

TURKISH DELIGHT HOLIDAYS
164B Heath Road, Twickenham, Middx. TW1 4BN
Tel: 01-891 5901 Telex: 925368 TDHOLS
ABTA 69608 ATOL 2047
1, 2, 3 week One / Two / Three Centre holidays in Bodrum, Türkbükü, Gümüslük, Ortakent, Gündogan, Turunc, Dalyan, Ölü Deniz, Patara, Kalkan, Kaş.
1 and 2 week luxury gulet cruises.
4 day coach trips to Cappadocia from Kalkan, Kaş, Patara or Ölü Deniz.
Fly-drive holidays, flight-only arrangements.

TURKISH VILLAS
35 Hanover Gardens, London SE11 5TN
Tel: 01-735 6037 ATOL 2042
A good selection of privately owned holiday homes to rent for one week and longer, from April to October in Türkbükü and Geris on the Bodrum Peninsula; on the south-west coast of Antalya and between Dikili and Ayvalık on the Northern Aegean Coast.
Tailor-made or accommodation-only service and fly-drive available, if preferred.

TURKISH WILDLIFE HOLIDAYS
The Grange, 8 Elmdon Park, Solihull, West Midlands B92 9EL
Tel: 021-742 5420 or 021-705 5535
Telex: 337000 JBESOL
14, 16 and 19 day adventure tours with hotel accommodation for small groups.
11, 16 and 19 day birdwatching tours – May, August and September (escorted small groups).
Sail treks. Underwater adventures. Fly-drive holidays.
Tailor-made winter holidays in Istanbul and Antalya (duration to suit clients).
Private small group tours arranged.
Flight-only and accommodation-only available.

TURQUOISE HOLIDAYS
35 D'Arblay Street, London W1V 3FE
Tel: 01-629 5908 or 01-491 2448   Telex: 269923 TURLON G
North London Office: 114 Green Lanes, London N16 9HE
Tel: 01-249 7792   ATOL 2158
1, 2 and 3 week One or Two Centre holidays in Istanbul, Şile, Kuşadası, Altınkum, Bodrum, Akyarlar, Güvercinlik, Marmaris, Dalyan, Kalkan, Kaş, Antalya, Side, Incekum.
Tailor-made winter holidays in Istanbul (any length).
Blue Cruises from Bodrum, Marmaris and Kaş.
Fly-drive and tailor-made holidays, flight-only arrangements.

UKEXPRESS TRAVEL SERVICES LTD.
Whitehall House, 41 Whitehall, London SW1A 2BY
Tel: 01-839 3303   Telex: 8956029   ABTA 60497   ATOL 1362
1 week holidays in Istanbul, 1 and 2 week holidays in Kuşadası, Bodrum, Marmaris, Kemer, Alanya, or combining one of the resorts with Istanbul, if two-centre preferred.
Coach tours: 2 week 'Grand Scenic' can be combined with Alanya.
1 week 'Best of Turkey', can be combined with Marmaris.
1 week 'Central Turkey', can be combined with Alanya.
1 week 'Eastern Turkey', can be combined with Alanya.

USIT CHARTERS LTD.
52 Grosvenor Gardens, London SW1W 0AG
Tel: 01-730 7285   Telex: 23472 USITUK   ATOL STAC LTD. 822
Special student charter flights to Istanbul from June to September inclusive.

VENTURA HOLIDAYS
125 Aldersgate Street, London EC1A 4JQ
Tel: London 01-250 1355   Telex: 295921 VENHOL G
Also at: 279 South Road, Sheffield S6 3TA
Tel: 0742 331100
88 Deansgate, Manchester M3 2ER
Tel: 061-834 5033   ATOL 2034
7 and 14 night holidays in Istanbul, Çeşme, Gümüldür, Kuşadası, Altınkum, Bodrum, Gümbet, Bitez, Turgutreis, Marmaris and Fethiye. Pansiyon, hotel and self-catering accommodation. Two-centres available.
7 night gulet cruises from Bodrum.
14 night Grand Circuit coach tour.
7 night Istanbul and North Aegean coach tour.
7 night Cappadocia and Mediterranean coach tour.
Fly-drive and tailor-made holidays. Flight-only, accommodation-only service.

WALLACE ARNOLD/GLOBAL TOURS
Gelderd Road, Leeds LS12 6DM
Tel: 0532 636456   Telex: 55482   ABTA 62242   ATOL 0316
8 and 15 day coach tours: Izmir, Canakkale, Bursa, Istanbul. Optional extension to Çeşme (8 days).

WAYMARK HOLIDAYS LTD.
295 Lillie Road, London SW6 7LL
Tel: 01-385 5015 or 01-358 3502   ATOL 624
14, 15 and 16 night trekking holidays in Eastern, Central and Southern Turkey.

WINGS
Broadway, Edgbaston, Fiveways, Birmingham B15 1BB
Tel: 021 643 2727   Telex: 335641   ABTA 35391   ATOL 169
7 and 14 night holidays in Kuşadasi, Bodrum, Gümbet, Side. Hotels and self-catering holidays.
Flight-only arrangements.

WORLD STEAM LTD.
3 Shadwell Grove, Radcliffe-on-Trent, Nottingham NG12 2ET
Tel: 06073 4714 or 0533 714815   Telex: 377494 MKLEIN
Self-catering and hotel holidays in Kalkan and Kuşadası, from May to October. Also, fly-drive.
Special interest: 100% steam hauled special trains with sleeping and restaurant cars. Two separate tours for steam enthusiasts (20.8.89-29.8.89 and 27.8.89-4.9.89).
1 week coach tours which can be linked with rail tour or beach holiday.
'The Anatolia-Tigris Express' (19.5.89-4.6.89). Special diesel-hauled train journey. Central, Eastern and Southern Turkey.

WORLDWIDE CHRISTIAN TRAVEL
50 Coldharbour Road, Redland, Bristol BS6 7NA
Tel: 0272 731840   Telex: 449017   ABTA 93522
10-15 day Religious and Historical Tours, mainly of Western Turkey.
Fly-drive and tailor-made holidays, flight-only and accommodation-only arrangements.

WINTER HOLIDAYS

AEGEAN TURKISH HOLIDAYS
53A Salusbury Road, London NW6 6NJ
Tel: 01-372 6902   Telex: 265260   ABTA 71773   ATOL 997
Holidays in Istanbul and Antalya.

AEGINA CLUB
25A Hills Road, Cambridge CB2 1NW
Tel: 0223 63256   Telex: 61684 AEGINA   ATOL 0262
3, 4 and 7 day breaks in Istanbul.
7 day holidays in Antalya and Side.
4 day tour of Bursa, Çanakkale, Troy.

ALLEGRO HOLIDAYS
15A Church Street, Reigate, RH2 0AA
Tel: 0737 221323   Telex: 919114 ALEGRO G
ABTA 12173   ATOL 1835
7, 10, 14 day holidays in Antalya, and Antalya/Istanbul two-centre.

AQUASPORT TOURS LTD.
181 Edward Street, Brighton BN2 2JB
Tel: 0273 685824
7 and 14 day individual hunting holidays based at Edremit, Marmaris, Antalya.

BEST YACHTING AND TOURISM
Kargi Marine, Hillier House, 509 Upper Richmond Road, London SW14 7EE
Tel: 01-873 3227   Telex: 9413819 HILHOU G
7-28 days and long-stay lets in villas on the South Coast.
7-21 days winter sailing from Göcek.

BLUESPOT TRAVEL LTD.
28 Maddox Street, London W1R 9PF
Tel: 01-408 0094   Telex: 297547 BLUSPT G   ATOL 2113
3, 4, 7, 10 days and flexible arrangements in Istanbul, Izmir and Antalya.
Two and multi-centre holidays can be arranged.

BOSPHORUS HOLIDAYS
Silver House, 31-35 Beak Street, London W1R 3LD
Tel: 01-437 7316   Telex: 296398 BOSPOR
3 nights to 3 months or longer. Istanbul, Izmir, Ankara, Bursa, Kayseri, Bolu, Erzurum, Kars and Mersin. Skiing, city breaks, thermal resorts, all tailor-made.

CELEBRITY HOLIDAYS AND TRAVEL
18 Frith Street, London W1V 5TS
Tel: 01-439 1961   Telex: 269304   ABTA 18659   ATOL 1469
3, 5, 7 and 14 days in Istanbul. 7 and 14 days in Side. Also two-centre Istanbul/Side and Istanbul/North Cyprus.

CLUB TURKEY
113 Upper Richmond Road, London SW15 2TL
Tel: 01-785 6389   Telex: 926631 CLUB TY G
ATOL: Agent for 754
7 and 14 night skiing holidays in Uludag and Bolu. À la carte skiing holidays in Erzurum. Two-centre holidays combining skiing and Istanbul or Antalya.
Tailor-made holidays.
School parties: skiing and educational 1/2 week tours.

CRUSADER CRUISING
14 Lissel Road, Simpson, Milton Keynes MK6 3AX
Tel: 0908 670346   Telex: 825264 SILBUS G
1, 2 and 3 week self-catering and hotel holidays in Bodrum and the surrounding area.

DELTASUN HOLIDAYS
58 Paddington Street, London W1M 3RR
Tel: 01-487 4503 or 01-935 9535   Telex: 265685 DSUN G
ATOL 2157
1, 2 and 3 week holidays in Istanbul, and 5-star hotel in Antalya.
Winter charter flights.

GOLDEN HORN TRAVEL
Golden House, 29 Gt. Pulteney Street, London W1R 3DD
Tel: 01-434 1962   Telex: 298287 GLDTR G
ABTA 31193   ATOL 1751
7, 10 and 14 day holidays in Antalya, Izmir and Side.
3, 7 and 14 day holidays in Istanbul.
Two-centre holidays: Istanbul with Antalya, Izmir or Side.

INTRA TRAVEL LTD.
121-122 Tottenham Court Road, London W1P 9NH
Tel: 01-383 7701   Telex: 928652 INTRA G   ATOL 2392
Long weekends in Istanbul and Izmir.
7 and 14 day holidays in Antalya.
Two-centre and tailor-made holidays available.

METAK HOLIDAYS
69/70 Welbeck Street, London W1M 7HA
Tel: 01-935 6961   Telex: 263188   ABTA 43858   ATOL 1116
3, 4, 5, 7, 10 and 14 day holidays in Istanbul and Antalya.
Two-centre holidays combining the two, or North Cyprus.

PAGE AND MOY LTD.
136-140 London Road, Leicester LE2 1EN
Tel: 0533 542000   Telex: 34583   ABTA 47026   ATOL 133
3 night holidays in Istanbul.
7 night Istanbul/Bursa.
Two-centre holiday.

REGENT HOLIDAYS UK LTD.
Regent House, 31a High Street, Shanklin, Isle of Wight
Tel: 0983 864212   Telex: 86197
3 to 28 night holidays in Istanbul, Izmir, Ankara and Antalya.

SAGA HOLIDAYS PLC
Saga Building, Middleburgh Square, Folkestone CT20 1AZ
Tel: 0800 300 456   Telex: 966331   ABTA 36888   ATOL 308
14, 21 and 28 night winter holidays in Alanya.

SAMSON TRAVEL LTD.
127 Kingsland High Street, London E8 2BP
Tel: 01-240 2687 or 01-240 5111   Telex: 927666 SAMSON G
ABTA 90755
3, 4, 7 and 14 day holidays in Istanbul, Izmir and Antalya.
Car hire, hotel arrangements, winter charter flights Christmas/ Easter.

SAVILE TRAVEL
32 Maddox Street, London W.1.
Tel: 01-499 5101   Telex: 269529   ATOL 2042
Winter holidays in Istanbul, Bursa, Troy-Çanakkale-Gelibolu, Antalya, Cappadocia.

STEEPWEST HOLIDAYS LTD.
449 Oxford Street, London W1R 1DA.
Tel: 01-629 2879   Telex: 297979   ABTA 55395   ATOL 1898
3, 7 and 14 night holidays in Istanbul, Antalya, Fethiye and Izmir.
Two-centre holidays.

SUNQUEST HOLIDAYS
Aldine House, Aldine Place, 141/142 Uxbridge Road, London W12.
Tel: 01-749 9933 or 01-749 9911   Telex: 22319
ABTA 57352   ATOL 754
3, 4 and 7 nights in Istanbul.
3, 4 and 7 night fly-drive and business travel.
Long-stay holidays: Antalya, Side, Kalkan, Kaş.
Two-centre holidays.
Short breaks.

THOMAS COOK FARAWAY HOLIDAYS
P.O. Box 36, Thorpe Wood, Peterborough PE9 3SN.
Tel: 0733 503203   ABTA: 20606   ATOL: 265
Great Little Journey Brochure:
5 days Istanbul/Bursa
4 days Istanbul

TOPAZ TRAVEL
7 Hartismere Road, London SW6 7TS.
Tel: 01-381 5189   Telex: 927526   ATOL Agents for 754B
3, 7 and 14 night holidays in Istanbul, Antalya and Kaş.
Also two-centre holidays.

TOURKEY TRAVEL
49 Pembridge Road, London W11 3HG.
Tel: 01-243 0383   Telex: 8953686   ATOL: Agents for 2167
3, 4, 7 and 14 night holidays in Istanbul, Bursa/Uludag, Yalova/Termal.
Whirling dervishes tour – December. 5 nights Istanbul/2 nights Konya.
Winter Wooden Horse Tours – 7 days.
Flight-only arrangements.

TRANSGLOBAL LTD.
64 Kenway Road, London SW5 0RD.
Tel: 01-244 8571   Telex: 938358 GLOBAL
'Turkey Panorama' 2 weeks winter coach tour of South-West and Central Turkey.

VENTURA HOLIDAYS
125 Aldersgate Street, London EC1A 4JQ.
Tel: 01-250 1355   Telex: 295921 VENHOL G   ATOL: 2034
3, 4, 7 and 14 day holidays in Istanbul, Bursa and Antalya.
Two-centres available.

SAILING AND YACHTING HOLIDAYS

ADVENTURE HOLIDAYS
10 Linden Park, Bangor, Co. Down.
Tel: 0247 473783
Specialise in yachting holidays in the Bodrum area.
Arrangements from Northern Ireland only.

ANCASTA YACHT CHARTER
Port Hamble Marina, Satchell Lane, Hamble, Southampton, Hants. SO3 5QD.
Tel: 0703 454565   Telex: 477879 ANCA G
From 1 week onwards, skippered and bareboat yacht charters from Marmaris and Göcek.
60 yachts from 60'.
Gulet cruising from Bodrum and Marmaris, 1 week or longer.
Tailor-made holidays.
Accommodation only arrangements.

AQUARIUS CRUISING
Western House, 9 Glandovey Terrace, Aberdovey, Gwynedd LL35 0EB.
Tel: 0654 72646   Telex: 35746 AQRSTL G
7, 14, 21 night, skippered and bareboat charters of yachts, catamarans, from Bitez.
Boats from 25' to 50', sleeping 2-10.

ARGOSY CRUISING
Harwood Bar, Great Harwood, Lancs BB6 7TE.
Tel: 0254 887692   Telex: 63422 ARGOSY G
1 week and longer charters (Marmaris – Fethiye – Kalkan – Kaş).
'Trinidad' 48' *luxury cruising ketch.*

BEST YACHTING AND TOURISM
Kargi Marine, Hillier House, 509 Upper Richmond Road, London SW14 7EE.
Tel: 01-873 3227   Telex: 9413819 HILHOU G
7 to 21 day skippered and bareboat charters from Göcek.
9-14m., 6-10 berth yachts.
7 to 21 day fully crewed gulet charters, 6-14 berths, from Bodrum, Marmaris, Göcek, Kaş and Antalya.
Flight and transfer arrangements available.

BLUE MOON CHARTERS
Blue Moon House, 92 Kingston Road, Portsmouth PO2 7PA.
Tel: 0705 662992   Telex: 86736 SOTEX G (Attn: BLMN)
1 or 2 weeks or more, crewed yacht or self-sail bareboats, all with 6 berths, from Marmaris.
Daily rate also available.

BLUESPOT TRAVEL LTD.
28 Maddox Street, London W1R 9PF.
Tel: 01-408 0094 or 01-409 3034   Telex: 297547 BLUSPT G
ATOL: 2113
1 and 2 week crewed gulets and bareboat charters from Bodrum and Marmaris. Guaranteed departures Blue Voyages.
MV 'Orient Express' Cruise: Venice/Istanbul/Kuşadasi and vice versa.

BOSPHORUS HOLIDAYS
Silver Street, 31-35 Beak Street, London W1R 3LD.
Tel: 01-437 7316   Telex: 296398
Turkish Maritime Lines cruises (Marmara, Aegean, Black Sea): One way, day return, or up to 10 days.

CANBERRA CRUISES
P and O Cruises Ltd., 77 New Oxford Street, London WC1A 1PP.
Tel: 01-831 1234   Telex: 885551
Cruise 903 (28 May-15 June) calling at Istanbul and Izmir, with optional coach tours.
Cruise 909 (19 August-3 September) calling at Izmir, with optional coach tours.

CRESTAR YACHT CHARTERS
Colette Court, 125/6 Sloane Street, London SW1X 9AU.
Tel: 01-730 9962   Telex: 918951 or 295054
Cruise Aegean and Mediterranean Turkey with crewed yachts. The vessels include more than 80 motor and sail yachts from 47'.
Tailor-made cruises.

CRUSADER CRUISING
14 Lissel Road, Simpson, Milton Keynes MK6 3AX.
Tel: 0908 670346   Telex: 825264 SILBUS
1, 2 and 3 week bareboat and skippered sail boats based at Bodrum (34' up), can be combined with accommodation for 'Stay-and-Sail' holidays.
1 or 2 week gulet cruising from Bodrum or Marmaris, can be combined with 'Stay-and-Sail' holidays.

DIVE AND SAIL
Commons Corner, Burleigh, Nr. Stroud, Glos. GL5 2SN.
Tel: 045 388 2267   Telex: 437269 SHARET G
1 to 2 week, weekly 'Live Aboard' dive charters on fully crewed and full equipped yachts. Unlimited diving, qualified instructors. Non-divers welcome.
'Learn to Dive' packages.
Flight-only arrangements.

FAIRWAYS AND SWINFORD TRAVEL
20 Upper Ground, London SE1 9PF.
Tel: 01-928 5044 or 01-261 1744   Telex: 8955803 SCN LDN
ABTA 28608   ATOL 491
Cruising in Turkish Waters on MV 'Orient Express', in conjunction with 1 week stay in Istanbul or Kuşadasi.

FALCON SAILING
33 Notting Hill Gate, London W11 3JQ.
Tel: 01-727 0232   Telex: 922889 (Attn: Sailing)
ABTA 68342   ATOL 1337
2 week Flotilla holidays or independent charter. 'Beneteau Oceanis 320' and 'Mirage 28' boats.

HALSEY MARINE LTD.
22 Boston Place, Dorset Square, London NW1 6HZ.
Tel: 01-724 1303   Telex: 265131 HALSEY G
Private yacht charter on fully crewed yachts from 45' to 120' plus, along the South West Turkish coast, from Izmir to Kekova.

ISLAND SAILING LTD.
The Port House, Port Solent, Portsmouth, Hampshire PO6 4TH.
Tel: 0705 210345   Telex: 86734 ISLAND G
ABTA 36996   ATOL 987
14 day flotilla and bareboat sailing from Marmaris, Datça and Fethiye.
Flight-only and accommodation-only service.

LANCASTER HOLIDAYS
26 Elmfield Road, Bromley, Kent BR1 1LR.
Tel: 01-697 8181   Telex: 8953010 LANAIR G
ABTA 3691X   ATOL 1960
14 night 'Turkey/Greece' cruising from Bodrum. Choice of Blue Cruises (7 and 14 days) from Bodrum, Marmaris, Fethiye, Kaş and Antalya. 3 night Mini-cruises from Fethiye and Kaş.
14 night 'Cruise and Stay' holidays.

LIZ FENNER WORLDWIDE YACHTING HOLIDAYS
35 Fairfax Place, London NW6 4EJ.
Tel: 01-328 1033   Telex: 262284 MONREF (Attn: 2641 Liz Fenner)
From 1 week to 2 months (or longer) holidays aboard crewed luxury sailing and motor yachts from 50' to 250'. From Bodrum, Marmaris, Göcek, Fethiye, Kaş and Antalya.
Tailor-made packages 35'-55' bareboat charters.

McCULLOCH MARINE CHARTER
60 Fordwych Road, London NW2 3TH.
Tel: 01-452 7509   Telex: 923753 Ref. 327
Agent for gulet specialists offering a large variety of fully crewed gulets and motor schooners. 6-12 berths for made-to-measure cruises around the South West coast of Turkey.
Flights and transfers arranged.

MV ORIENT EXPRESS
Suite 200, Hudsons Place, Victoria Station, London SW1V 1JL.
Tel: 01-834 8122   Telex: 914840 OELDN G
Venice – Piraeus – Istanbul – Kuşadasi – Patmos – Katakolon – Venice (7 nights). Weekly Saturday departures from Venice March-October 1989.
Stopover journeys available.
Vehicle space available.

RAINBOW SAILING LTD.
Cardinal House, Church Row, Wernffrwd, Swansea.
Tel: 0792 467813   Telex: 94015991 RAIN G
Any number of weeks' bareboat and skippered charter on 29' to 40' Beneteau yachts, from Marmaris.

SAGA HOLIDAYS plc
The Saga Building, Middelburg Square, Folkestone, Kent CT20 1AZ.
Tel: 0800 300 456   Telex: 966331   ABTA 36888   ATOL 308
3 Cruises: 'Golden Fleece', 'Homeric Cruise' and 'Grand Cruise', visiting Kuşadasi.

SERENISSIMA TRAVEL LTD.
21 Dorset Square, London NW1 6QG.
Tel: 01-730 9841 or 723 6556
Telex: 914032/28441   ABTA 54693   ATOL 883B
Cruising in the Aegean on board M/V 'Serenissima Tura'.

SUNDOWN MARINE YACHT CHARTERS
Sundown House, Rectory Lane, Woodmansterne, Surrey SM7 3PP.
Tel: 0737 551271/2   Telex: 8956867 SUNGRP G
A full range of yacht charter holidays (any duration) in bareboat, skippered and crewed yachts from 28' to 155', Marmaris, Bodrum, Fethiye and along the coast.
Specialists in gulet cruises.
Tailor-made packages. All travel arrangements made.

SUNSAIL CLUBS
The Port House, Port Solent, Portsmouth, Hants PO6 4TH
Tel: 0705 219827   Telex: 86734 ISLAND G
ABTA 36996   ATOL 987
Watersports and Sailing Club holidays in the Marmaris and Bodrum areas.
Flight-only and accommodation-only arrangements.

SUNQUEST HOLIDAYS
Aldine House, Aldine Place, 141/142 Uxbridge Road, London W12.
Tel: 01-749 9933   Telex: 22319   ABTA 57352   ATOL 754
7 or 14 night yachting holidays from Bodrum. Agents for Turkish Maritime Lines – all destinations.
MV 'Orient Express': Venice/Istanbul/Kuşadasi.
14 night 'Turquoise Cruise'.

SWAN HELLENIC CRUISES
77 New Oxford Street, London WC1A 1PP.
Tel: 01-831 1234 (Res.) or 01-831 1515 (Adm.)   Tlelex: 88851
ABTA 27427   ATOL 0307
A large number of Mediterranean cruises on the 'Orpheus', many of which call at various Turkish ports, from Sinop to Mersin.

TEMPLECRAFT YACHT CHARTERS LTD.
33 Grand Parade, Brighton BN2 2QA.
Tel: 0273 695094   Telex: 94013292 TYCL   ATOL 2149
1 to 4 week skippered and bareboat charters (31' to 51' yachts) available from Marmaris, Göcek, Antalya and Fethiye.
Tailor-made arrangements.

TFC CRUISE LINES
49 Whitcomb Street, London WC2.
Tel: 01-930 7541   Telex: 946102   ABTA 72719
Cruises on 'Achille Lauro' calling at Istanbul, Izmir, Kuşadasi.

TOP YACHT CHARTER LTD.
Andrew Hill Lane, Hedgerley, Bucks SL2 2UW.
Tel: 02814 6636   Telex: 23152 MONREF G   ATOL 1761
2 weeks or more from Bodrum and Göcek: 26 yachts from 30'-49' for bareboat charter from Bodrum to Göcek.
46' to 60' sailing yachts with skipper and hostess.
Fully crewed 'gulets', to take 6-12 guests.
Flights on Wednesdays from Gatwick and Manchester to Dalaman.
Coach transfers. Flight-only arrangements.

VIAMARE TRAVEL
33 Mapesbury Road, London NW2 4HT.
Tel: 01-452 8231/2 or 01-452 0692/3   Telex: 9413206 MARE G
Summer ferry services Italy to Turkey: Ancona – Patras – Heraklion – Kuşadasi.
Year round ferry crossing Rhodes – Marmaris.

YACHTCLUB CHARTER COMPANY LTD.
307 New Kings Road, London SW6 4RF.
Tel: 01-731 0826   Telex: 268867 YACHTC G   ATOL 2272
1-4 week bareboat charters of 28' to 42' yachts.
Skipper also available.
Large variety of Turkish gulets complete with crew.
Sailings from Bodrum and Fethiye. April to October.
Daytime flights with coach transfers.
Tailor-made holidays, flight-only and accommodation-only arrangements.

YACHT CRUISING ASSOCIATION
The Port House, Port Solent, Portsmouth, Hampshire PO6 4TH.
Tel: 0705 219844   Telex: 869110 YCA G
ABTA 36996   ATOL 987
14-day flotilla sailing holidays along the South Coast (Kaş, Kekova), and Bodrum area.

INDEX

Alanya **107**, 15
Altinkum **93**, 16
Antalya . . . **105**, 15, 125
Antiphellos (see Kaş)
Aphrodisias **117**
Aspendos **124**, 106
Ayvalik **89**

Beldibi **105**
Bergama (see Pergamon)
Bodrum . **94**, 119, 99, 15,
13 129

Çaliş **101**
Çanakkale **110**
Caunos **121**
Cavus **104**
Çeşme **90**

Dalyan **121**
Datça **97**
Demre **124**, 104
Didyma **119**, 93

Ephesus **113**
Erythrai **90**

Fethiye . . . **101**, 99, 13
Foça **89**

Gallipoli **110**
Gümbet **95**, 94

Gümüşlük **97**
Güvercinlik **97**
Güzelçamli **91**

Halikarnassus (see
Bodrum)
Hierapolis (see
Pamukkale)

Içmeler **99**, 16
Ilica **90**
Istanbul **73**

Kadinlar **91**
Kalkan **103**
Kapitas **104**
Kaş . . **123**, 95, 102, 103
Kekova **124**, 104
Kemer **105**
Kilyos **88**, 73
Knidos **97**
Kuşadasi . . . **91**, 113

Letoon **122**

Manavgat **127**
Manisa **113**
Map of resorts **86**
Marmaris . . **98**, 49, 121
Meryemana **116**
Miletus **118**
Myra **104**, 124

Ölü Deniz **101**, 15
Oren **88**

Pamukkale **117**
Patara **102**, 16
Pergamon **112**, 89
Perge . . . **129**, 106, 107
Priene **118**

Sardis **112**
Selçuk (see Ephesus)
Side . . **106**, 126, 15, 107
Şile **87**, 73

Teos **90**
Termessos **125**, 106
Troy **111**
Turgutries **97**

Xanthos **122**